HOW TO BE A GREAT SALES PROFESSIONAL

Nido R. Qubein

ALSO BY NIDO R. QUBEIN

BOOKS

ACHIEVING PEAK PERFORMANCE

GET THE BEST FROM YOURSELF

HOW TO BE A GREAT COMMUNICATOR

HOW TO GET ANYTHING YOU WANT

STAIRWAY TO SUCCESS

THE TIME IS NOW, THE PERSON IS YOU

CASSETTES

COMMUNICATE LIKE A PRO

HOW TO POSITION YOURSELF FOR SUCCESS

HOW TO SELL, SERVE AND SUCCEED

HOW TO SUCCEED IN BUSINESS AND IN LIFE

MARKETING PROFESSIONAL SERVICES

NIDO QUBEIN LIVE!

VIDEOS

PERSONAL AND PROFESSIONAL EXCELLENCE

THE ART OF EFFECTIVE COMMUNICATION

THE CRESTCOM MANAGEMENT SERIES

THE MAGIC IS IN THE MIX

THE MIRACLE IS IN THE MIX

THE WINNING DIFFERENCE

Copyright © 1998 by Nido R. Qubein

Library of Congress Cataloging in Publication Data

ISBN 0-939975-13-0

For quantity purchases of this book contact:

Executive Press
806 Westchester Drive
P. O. Box 6008
High Point, NC 27262 USA
(336)889-3010, Facsimile (336)885-3001

Printed in the United States of America

**To Mariana,
With Love**

Acknowledgments

To God from whom all my blessings have come, I owe everything I am and everything I have.

To my close and dear friends who accepted me, guided me, and loved me throughout my journey, I owe deep gratitude.

To my loyal clients who've stuck with me through all these years—and who entrusted their people and meetings to me, I owe unending appreciation.

To my speaker buddies, my hometown (High Point, North Carolina) pals, my staff, my family, and my business partners, I express unconditional love. You've meant so much to me.

To the millions who invested in my books, cassettes, videos, and seminars across America and the world, my work simply could not have been enhanced and nurtured without you. Thank you, thank you, thank you.

Introducing Nido Qubein

Nido Qubein is chairman of an international management consulting firm serving clients across the U.S. and in a dozen other countries. He specializes in conceptualizing, creating, and delivering fully integrated behavioral systems for employees and their leaders.

Nido is a partner in several companies and serves on the board of many universities, corporations, and community organizations. He has been the recipient of many honors, including a Doctor of Laws degree, the Ellis Island Congressional Medal of Honor, the Cavett (known as the Oscar of the speaking profession), the Sales and Marketing International Hall of Fame, and Citizen of the Year in High Point, North Carolina, where he resides.

He speaks each year to more than a hundred audiences at conventions, sales meetings, and executive conferences. He has written many books and recorded scores of audio and video programs, which have been translated into several languages.

You can reach Nido Qubein at: Creative Services, Inc. • P. O. Box 6008 • High Point • NC 27262 USA • Telephone 336-889-3010 • Facsimile 336-885-3001.

Introduction

———

How To Be A Great Sales Professional

*Sell Your Products, Serve Your Customers,
and Succeed in a Competitive World*

By Nido R. Qubein

$\mathbf{A}$ sales career can be your route to the good life or your sentence to a life of frustration. The choice is up to you. It has nothing to do with the luck of the draw or the roll of the dice. It has everything to do with the way you think and perform as a salesperson.

In no other calling is your success tied so directly to your performance. If you're a manager or a salaried executive, your income is usually based on someone else's estimate of how well you perform.

If you're in sales, it is related directly to your actual performance. If you make a lot of sales, you make a lot of money. If sales are lean, so are your earnings.

Some people assume that selling is a natural talent; you either have it or you don't. If you have it, they reason, all you have to do is find the right product, pick up your briefcase, and go knocking on doors. Your natural charm and persuasiveness are all you need to start the orders rolling in and the good times rolling on.

Such people generally end up frustrated and eager to strike out in other careers. Or they wise up and learn selling savvy.

For selling, no matter what your level of talent, is not just an art to be possessed; it is also a discipline to be learned. You can learn it, and by putting your learning into practice you can achieve the good life you've dreamed of.

A talented pianist can learn to play quite well on her own, and may become the life of the party among her friends. But if she wants to achieve professional success, she has to study. She has to learn the techniques and put them into practice.

A talented baseball player may be able to walk off the sandlots into a major-league training camp and occasionally connect with the ball. But to make it to the big time, he needs coaching in the finer points of the batter's trade. He needs to learn the techniques and he must put them into practice. Many a player of mediocre talent has outshone more gifted performers by becoming a student of the game and by showing sheer hustle.

The same goes for sales. You can hit the road without training and without preparation and occasionally make a sale. But to make a living—a good living—you need to learn the techniques and practice them.

This book will give you the techniques. You have to supply the practice—and the hustle. But if you follow the suggestions contained in these pages, you're going to hear a lot more people say "yes" to your sales presentation, and you're going to make a lot more money.

In the very first chapter, you'll learn the crucial factor that separates winning salespeople from losing salespeople: Losers do things right, but winners do the right things.

The first "right thing" you'll need to do is to position yourself in the eyes of your potential customers. People aren't likely to buy from you if they don't have confidence in you. You'll learn how to earn this confidence by presenting yourself as an expert in your field.

You'll also learn about the two critical dimensions of selling: the macro dimension, which deals with the big picture, and the micro dimension, which deals with all the minute details that keep you in control of each selling situation. You'll learn how to master both to boost your selling effectiveness.

Next you'll learn to add power to your persuasion by employing the seven *P*'s of selling: your *p*ower to *p*ersuade *p*lenty of *p*rospects to *p*urchase your *p*roducts at a *p*rofit. You'll learn to use persuasion, not pressure or manipulation, to get a sale.

To be successful in sales, you must be an accomplished communicator. Some of us are naturally glib and some of us are more reserved, but all of us can learn to get our messages across effectively. For a salesperson, communicating means making it clear to your prospects what you are offering and how it will benefit them.

The most important commodity a salesperson has to deal with is time. Using time wisely enables you to work smarter and not just harder. In this book, you'll learn two simple steps that will enable you to make maximum use of your time.

Most salespeople decide what they want to sell, then try to talk people into buying it. These are the people who remain mired in mediocrity.

Savvy salespeople find out what people want, and then help them to get it. As you read this book, you'll learn how to follow this approach to sales success.

You'll learn to boost your sales by asking key questions. You can do this without grilling your prospects. In fact, you'll learn that the most important questions are not the ones you ask your prospect.

What are the questions and whom do you ask? Stay tuned and learn.

As you read further, you'll learn the value of focusing your sales presentation for maximum effect. You'll learn how research, planning, and practice can focus your efforts the way a laser focuses light.

Your presentation is the crucial point in the sales process. With it, you either make a sale or you lose it.

We'll examine two myths connected with the sales presentation.

Myth No. 1: The sale is up to the prospect; success depends upon whether the prospect likes the product and wants to buy it.

Myth No. 2: A positive attitude will clinch the sale.

We'll replace these two myths by outlining four ways to move the prospect to a buying decision.

Every salesperson knows that prospects have objections. The difference between the pros and the amateurs is this: Amateurs look upon objections as obstacles to be overcome. Pros look upon them as positive indications of the reasons a particular prospect refuses to buy. Then, they eliminate the reasons one by one. With the reasons gone, the sale is likely to be made.

Finally, we'll take you through the process of closing.

Closing the sale is what brings home the bread; if you don't close you don't eat, and you don't enjoy all the other components of the good life. When you come to the end of the book, you'll learn some time-tested techniques that will enable you to close a higher percentage of your sales, allowing you to follow up for even greater future sales.

Selling is one of the most exciting and rewarding careers you can pursue. It provides you with constant challenge. The rewards can be constant, too, if you learn the savvy approach detailed in this book.

If you're serious about a sales career, this book will provide you with the key to success and prosperity. If you're already in sales but disappointed at your progress thus far, don't give up until you've read this book and applied what you've learned.

The techniques have been tested and proved.

Follow them to fulfill your dreams of success.

Contents

Contents

Separating the Pros From the Amateurs

What makes a successful salesperson?

I've often asked that question at seminars, and the answers have been all over the ball park.

"You've got to have the right product," some say.

It helps. But we've all known salespeople who went broke trying to move superb products and others who could make fortunes selling ice cream on an iceberg. A really good salesperson can rack up more sales with a mediocre product than a mediocre salesperson can make with the greatest product in the world.

"You've got to make plenty of sales calls," others say. "The more calls you make, the more sales you'll get."

As a general rule, that's true, but it doesn't go far enough. If you think about it, the more passes a quarterback throws, the more passes he'll complete. But a quarterback who completes three out of four passes will put points on the board much more regularly than one who completes one out of four, even though both may throw the same number of times. A baseball player who hits .350 will cross the plate much more frequently than one who hits .200, even though both take the same number of swings.

Similarly, a salesperson's success doesn't depend on the number of calls. It depends on the number of sales. An effective salesperson and an ineffective salesperson may make the same number of calls, but it's the effective one who eats steak and lobster instead of hamburger.

Still others say, "You've got to master the mechanics." That helps, too. But mastering the mechanics won't put you on top of the sales charts unless you master the *right* mechanics.

The Difference Between Excellence and Mediocrity

That brings us to the true distinction between a top salesperson and a mediocre performer: Mediocre people do things right, but winners do the right things. Hard-working salespeople who focus on doing things right may fail. Those who focus on doing the right things become top performers.

The difference is enormous. You can memorize hundreds of selling scripts and scores of closing techniques and polish them to perfection. But if you don't really understand human nature—if you don't know why prospects do what they do—you won't be able to do enough of the right things to succeed as a salesperson.

Take the Pragmatic Approach

Selling savvy means knowing how to read people; how to control the sales process; and how to bring people to a buying decision. It's sticking to what works and staying away from what doesn't work. A simple, pragmatic approach to selling is what separates the winners from the losers in the exciting profession of sales and marketing.

It's that kind of approach that will be outlined in this book. It will introduce you to simple but highly effective techniques that have helped hundreds of thousands of salespeople around the world to boost their selling power.

NAVIGATING THE CHANGED SALES ENVIRONMENT

In today's market, as in none before, it is crucial that we learn selling savvy. The sales environment has changed radically in four distinct ways:

Separating the Pros From the Amateurs

(1) *Customers are better-educated, more sophisticated, and more value-conscious.*

In other words, they are harder to please; they want more for their money.

Think about your own demands as a consumer. You insist on quality goods and efficient service. You don't want some slick con artist trying to trick you into buying a product or service you don't want or need. And you don't want to be abandoned after the sale.

You expect follow-up service. If something goes wrong, you want to know that the salesperson and the company are going to stand behind the sale.

This means that salespeople have to stay on top of their markets. They have to be knowledgeable about the products and services they are selling. And they have to be honest and sincerely interested in helping their customers find value and derive satisfaction.

Customers expect more from us than ever before.

(2) *Competition is stiffer.*

Customers now have so many options that price will always be the deciding factor—unless you can offer a strong differential advantage.

With companies producing similar products at similar cost, it's getting tougher every day to offer substantially lower prices than the competition does.

That means that you have to offer something that sets you apart from all the other salespeople who are trying to get your customers to buy from them. You have to provide quicker service, more up-to-date product knowledge, and better follow-up.

It's not enough to provide products and service as good as those of your competitors. Yours have to be better—a lot better. Moreover, your customers must acknowledge the superiority of your products and services, and the object of your presentation should be to lead them toward that recognition and acknowledgment.

If you can't lead your customers to that acknowledgment, you won't get the sale no matter how good your product. Your success in selling depends less and less on the product you are selling, and more and more on your skills as a salesperson.

(3) *Technology is rapidly replacing peddlers.*

People are buying more through direct mail. And such media as interactive television and the Internet are making it possible to buy almost anything you want by pressing a button or clicking a mouse.

Companies are no longer looking for peddlers to handle items that are much easier to sell by phone or through the mail. In many cases, they're setting up self-service systems that can be operated by clerks.

Of course, there are plenty of very good opportunities for really sharp salespeople who can sell with power and skill.

To be successful as a salesperson, you must find ways to distinguish yourself from the inexpensive clerks and the commonplace peddlers. You must rise to the challenge with proficient skills, depth of knowledge, and a positive attitude.

(4) *Time has become a priceless commodity—for salespeople and for their customers.*

Prospects don't want salespeople wasting their time.

And if you're serious about becoming successful, you don't have time to wander around showing your products or services to anyone who will look at them.

To survive in today's volatile marketplace, you need a clear and effective strategy. You need the skills to implement that strategy. And you need the know-how to make that strategy work for you.

When you acquire and apply these things, you're demonstrating selling savvy.

FIVE INGREDIENTS TO SALES SUCCESS

What do we mean by selling savvy?

The answer lies in five ingredients that are vital to your success as a salesperson:

(1) *Selling savvy is understanding the selling process well enough to approach it as a highly educated professional.*

You have to understand the selling process so well that you don't have to stop and think about what you are doing at any given time. When it's time to close a sale, you can sense it intuitively, and you know how to go about it.

When a prospect is becoming uncomfortable with the selling situation, you know how to deal with those negative feelings.

I'm talking about developing the same kind of instinct for selling that cats have for always landing on their feet. If you hold a cat by its legs six feet off the ground and you let go, that cat is going to land on its feet.

If you do the same thing, but hold the cat only four inches off the ground, that cat will still land on its feet. It has a built-in sense for landing right-side-up.

Professional salespeople have the same kind of built-in sense for knowing what to do, what to say, and how to react in any sales situation. They have conditioned their minds to operate on the basics of selling. It's second-nature to them.

(2) *Selling savvy is understanding people well enough to influence them to buy.*

You have to be able to read your prospects well enough to know how to deal with each of them as a unique individual. That means understanding their personality types, their buying patterns, and the way they perceive their needs. It means knowing people well enough to influence their buying decisions.

Selling savvy is listening to what people are saying and to what they are ***not*** saying. It's knowing where your prospects are coming from so you can determine what sales approaches will work best with them.

(3) *Selling savvy is knowing how to execute.*

That means knowing how to get the job done. It's knowing how to take all your training and all the skills you have developed and put them to work for you in the real world of selling.

That takes guts. You risk rejection and failure. But it's the only way you can ever become good enough at the game to win consistently.

(4) *Selling savvy means developing street smarts.*

Street smarts is that instinctive intelligence you develop by observing and interacting with people. It doesn't come to you instantly and effortlessly. You have to cultivate it by going into your world of prospects and studying their likes and dislikes, their motives, and their responses.

You demonstrate your street smarts by the way you present yourself to prospects, by the kinds of questions you ask, and by your sense of timing.

You can sense when someone doesn't know what's going on. If you go to a lawyer, you can tell by the questions and comments you hear whether you've picked the right one.

The same is true of salespeople. People can sense when you are bluffing and when you know what you are talking about.

People with selling savvy have a confidence born of knowledge and experience. This shows up in everything you do.

(5) *Selling savvy is having the self-discipline to carry out every detail of your strategy all day, every day.*

Savvy salespeople keep one eye on the big picture and the other on every minute detail that's necessary to get the job done.

If you must make ten cold calls every day to keep a solid customer base, then you do it. If it takes you all night to make some final revisions on a proposal for a hot prospect, then you do it.

You do whatever it takes to implement your sales strategy and reach your goals.

How to Become a Totally Professional Salesperson

To become successful in today's volatile marketplace, you have to become a totally professional salesperson.

When you see the word "professional," what do you think of? A doctor? A lawyer? An educator?

When you go to a doctor, you are looking for a medical expert who can help cure your illness or prevent you from getting sick in the first place. You expect that doctor to help you solve a problem.

The doctor has the skills, experience, and professional manner that instill confidence in you, the patient.

Similarly, you expect a lawyer to be familiar with the law and to have the skills to serve you ably as an advocate.

Moreover, you expect these people to be well-rounded, well-educated people—at ease with all levels of society.

Qualities That Set Salespeople Apart

Whether they're doctors, lawyers, or salespeople, there's a quality about professionals that sets them apart from the ordinary run of people. Being a professional is not a matter of what you know or what you can do; it involves the basic question of what you are. Once you become a professional you are a changed person.

Professional salespeople, of course, must acquire skills quite different from those of doctors, lawyers, and educators. But there are some characteristics that all professionals hold in common.

Acquiring Manners and Taste

Professionals are looked up to as people of manners, culture, and good taste. Once you have acquired professional and cultural polish, you have become a different person, and you won't go back to what you were before.

Acquiring culture and polish means exposing yourself to new people, new places, and new experiences. Travel itself is broadening. If you've ever visited a foreign country, you have expanded the horizon of your mind. You understand the world in a different way, and it shows subtly in the way you interact with people. You not only know how things are done at home; you also know how they're done in other parts of the world, and you may have found some things that work there better than they do here. In the global sales climate, that can give you a competitive edge.

Author Robert Louis Stevenson advised: "If you can't travel, read about new places." Your public library will have illustrated books on other places, and probably a number of videotapes as well.

You can stretch your experiences in other areas as well. If you like a certain kind of music, by all means enjoy it. But occasionally listen to other types of music. You may find that you can enjoy Beethoven as well as the Beatles; Rachmaninoff as well as Manilow.

As you expand your tastes, you will find yourself comfortable with a broader segment of society, which means that you will be expanding your universe of sales prospects. Your new knowledge will give you a great deal more self-confidence, which will help you make a more favorable impression on a wider variety of people.

Cultivating the Art of Conversation

In social situations, you'll find it easier to approach strangers if you're prepared to talk on a variety of subjects. You'll be better prepared if you've read a good book, seen a good movie, or learned something new from newspaper and television reports.

Being cultured doesn't mean that you have to recognize all of Beethoven's symphonies after the first few bars or be able to tell at a glance what century a particular painting belongs to. But it helps to know something about the fine arts and to know enough to hold your own in conversations involving contemporary culture.

Americans increasingly are turning their leisure-time attention to the arts, and salespeople who can discuss poetry, music, literature, painting, and the dance as well as the Super Bowl, the World Series, and the NBA championships, will enhance their professional images and will appeal to a broader universe of prospects.

Professional salespeople are educated. That doesn't mean that you must have an advanced degree to be a good salesman. It does mean that you must develop broad reading habits, keeping well abreast of current events and business trends. Your ability to do that will give you a competent manner that will build confidence in your prospects.

PROFESSIONALS VERSUS WORKERS

I often draw the distinction between a person with a worker mentality and a person with a professional mentality.

Workers tolerate their jobs as burdens to be endured for the sake of putting food on their tables and roofs over their heads.

Professionals see their jobs as rewarding components of their lives. Their careers and their personal lives complement and support each other. Their jobs are part of who they are.

Workers wait to be told what to do. They don't reach out for new responsibility, because they don't want responsibility. They take care of their own immediate tasks without worrying about how their tasks affect others in the organization. In fact, they don't see themselves as part of the organization. They see the organization as an outside entity that may have a negative or positive impact on their lives. They refer to it in the third person: as "it" or "them," and not as "we." The organization is something they have to respond to, although they're not a part of it.

Professionals see themselves as part of the organization. To them, the organization is "we." When it succeeds, they succeed. When it suffers reverses, they feel the reverses.

People look up to professionals because they recognize them as being good at what they do. They're good because they've walked the extra mile toward excellence. They absorb information about their chosen fields, and they share their knowledge with others. They're jealous of their images and are always careful to avoid compromising them. To be a professional, you have to look like a pro, communicate like a pro, and exude the confidence of a pro. You must set a high standard for yourself and never allow yourself to fall below that standard.

Here are some characteristics that will enable you to distinguish the pros from the amateurs:

(1) *Professional people have specialized knowledge and skills.*

Professional salespeople, like any other group of professionals, need extra knowledge and skills to enable them to render valuable service to their customers.

They take advantage of every available opportunity to learn as much as they can about their businesses, their products, their companies, their professions, and their competition. They know that only then can they adequately look after their customers' concerns.

Professional salespeople are constantly sharpening their sales skills. They have confidence in their knowledge and experience, but they recognize that sharp edges grow dull unless they are constantly honed. They also know that as the competition gets keener, their skills must get keener if they expect to keep ahead.

(2) *Professionals maintain unique relationships with clients.*

Professional salespeople know that their customers rely on them for valuable information they need to make important decisions. And they are deeply committed to delivering value to their customers.

Professional salespeople value the unique relationships they hold with their clients and seek to establish trust and respect.

The real pros in selling build trust through dependable and cheerful service, loyalty, and sincerity, and by proving their professional competence.

You can always identify the professional salespeople, because their customers buy from them again and again.

(3) *Professionals render valuable service.*

If your service isn't valuable, people won't pay for it. So the pros look for ways to be valuable to their customers.

Selling is a crucial function to any business, and most companies are glad to pay high commissions, salaries, or bonuses to get it done right. And most customers recognize that a part of their purchase price goes to pay salespeople.

(4) *Professionals are self-managed but accountable.*

A mark of professionalism in selling is recognizing that the salesperson is accountable to the company—and to the customer.

A company has every right to hold its salespeople accountable for their actions. And salespeople who are really successful don't make false claims or promises to customers just to get them to buy.

Successful salespeople are self-managed. They don't need bosses to plan their schedules, organize their presentations, and push them out of the door each day to call on prospects. Their own self-respect demands that they work hard, that they show initiative, and that they be persistent. It also demands that they operate ethically and with integrity.

(5) *Professional people have positive attitudes.*

Sales professionals maintain positive self-images and strong feelings of self-confidence. They are resourceful in finding prospects and in solving problems. They have a sense of responsibility.

And professional salespeople are open to learn and eager to grow. They are constantly reaching out to tackle new challenges.

Those are the marks of a professional salesperson. They provide some valuable clues as to what it takes to be successful in the exciting selling profession.

From Mediocrity to Excellence via Education

But becoming a truly professional salesperson goes beyond developing a handful of professional attributes.

Professionalism also means accepting the challenge to go beyond career mediocrity to personal and professional excellence.

It means going beyond training to education.

Stanley Marcus, the genius behind the Neiman-Marcus department stores, once said, "You don't train salespeople; you train dogs and bears. You educate salespeople."

Training has to do with knowledge and skills—both of which are vitally important. But education has to do with understanding how to apply your knowledge and skills to every selling situation. Training teaches you how to do things well, but education teaches you how to think.

Working Hard and Working Smart

Professionalism means going beyond trying to meet quotas. It means becoming an effective performer. It calls for working hard, but also working smart. You aren't just interested in completing tasks; you want to see results.

Professionalism entails going beyond peddling products to becoming your customer's consultant. To do that, you must focus less on spouting information and more on solving problems for your clients.

A professional goes beyond doing a job and focuses on building a professional career. That includes having a professional mindset. It's thinking of yourself as a professional and projecting an image that makes others think of you that same way.

This projection of an image—portraying yourself as a professional in the minds of your customers—is what we refer to as positioning.

In the next chapter, you'll learn how to position yourself as a professional and set yourself up for success in the exciting world of sales.

———

CHECK YOUR SELLING SAVVY

I. Name four ways in which the sales environment has changed, making selling savvy all the more important:

    (1) _____

    (2) _____

    (3) _____

    (4) _____

II. List the five key ingredients of selling savvy:

(1) _____

(2) _____

(3) _____

(4) _____

(5) _____

III. List five qualities that mark true professionals:

(1) _____

(2) _____

(3) _____

(4) _____

(5) _____

Positioning Yourself as a Selling Professional

Let's face it: Most decision makers don't sit around all day drumming their fingers on their desks and saying, "Gee, I wish a nice salesperson would show up and give me a presentation."

Most of them have busy schedules, and the last thing they want is for an amateur salesperson to interrupt their day to try to sell them something they're not aware that they need.

You're familiar with this scenario:

Joe Armtwister wanders into a large business office and asks to see the company president.

The receptionist looks at Joe with all the charm of a drill sergeant and asks, "Do you have an appointment?"

"No, I don't," Joe answers, "But I have something very important to discuss with the president."

The receptionist gives him that cold look and says, "I'm sorry, he's tied up all day."

And he'll be tied up tomorrow and the next day, too, when it comes to seeing Joe.

Positioning to Penetrate the Executive Suite

Yet, some salespeople have no trouble penetrating the barriers to the executive suite. Executives are glad to schedule appointments with them, and make them welcome when they arrive.

What do they have that Joe Armtwister doesn't have?

It's called *positioning.*

Joe Armtwister has positioned himself as an inept nuisance.

Position Yourself as a Competent Pro

To avoid Joe's fate, you need to position yourself as a competent pro. You need to be someone decision makers *want* to see, because they value your expertise; because they recognize you as a person of integrity; because they believe you're on their side; because they know that you know things that can help them run their businesses more smoothly and profitably.

In this chapter, we'll discuss the meaning of positioning and how it works. Most important, we'll explore methods of positioning yourself so that people will sit up and take notice of what you have to say.

By *positioning,* I mean presenting yourself as an expert in your field. You present yourself as a professional, much as doctors and lawyers do. You position yourself as a valuable resource—a person your prospects would not dare pass up an opportunity to see.

The way great salespeople position themselves is the biggest single factor in their ability to get appointments with key decision makers, even in many of the world's most successful companies.

DON'T BE A GENERIC SALESPERSON

Let's look at how it works.

The next time you're in a supermarket, notice how the customers react to brand-name products as opposed to generic products.

Most brand-name products are attractively packaged. Elaborate signs call attention to bargains. "Impulse items" seem to jump into shopping carts.

But far back in the corner of a low-traffic area, you'll find a small, jumbled-up rack of generic products in drab gray-and-black packages. The labels read simply, "Beans" or "Crackers." Nothing about those generic packages makes you want to buy them. It's almost as if the store manager is apologizing for even selling them at all.

These products are often 30% to 50% cheaper than their brand-name competitors, although they may be identical to the merchandise with the well-known names and the fancy labels.

But notice how few of those generic products end up in the shopping carts lined up at the cash registers. People just don't buy them.

Why don't people buy those high-quality products with the plain labels?

The difference lies in the positioning. The way they are packaged and presented has a profound effect on shopper decisions.

Think of a few examples.

Two pairs of blue jeans on the sales rack look identical except for one thing: One has a designer label on the hip; one has no label at all.

The quality and overall appearance may be the same, but the customers will buy the label and pay a premium price for it.

A man feels better in a Brooks Brothers suit, even though another suit in the same style made from the same material may be available for considerably less.

Become a Brand-Name Salesperson

Some products have positioned themselves so that when people think of the commodity, they think of that brand name. When people think of pineapple, they think of Dole; when they think of inexpensive cameras, they think of Kodak; when they think of facial tissues, they think of Kleenex; when they think of corn flakes, they think of Kellogg's; when they think of sewing machines, they think of Singer. People will buy products bearing these names more readily than they will buy products with lesser-known labels or with no labels at all. The reason is *positioning.*

It's the same way in personal selling. Your "position" is the way your customers and prospects perceive you and perceive what you are selling. It's what they think about you and your product or service.

Some salespeople are "generic." They may have good products and good prices, but to the prospects, they come across as run-of-the-mill. When they come calling, the decision maker has the feeling, "I've heard that pitch before and I don't need to hear it again."

Others are brand-name salespeople. Their prospects see them as people of substance selling high-value products. "Brand-name" salespeople outsell their "generic" competitors 20 to 1.

MAKE YOURSELF IMPORTANT

If you have several people who want to talk to you at once, which one will be the first to get your attention?

You're likely to choose the one who is the most important to you at the moment. That's human nature, whether you're a parent with three children shouting "Mom!" or "Dad!" or a business executive with three salespeople waiting in your reception area.

To get the executive's ear, you have to position yourself as someone who has something important to say. Ask yourself a series of questions to determine how well you're positioned for access to the buyer's office:

(1) *"How would my prospects and customers describe me to someone else?"*

Would they use such words as *pushy, obnoxious, abrasive,* and *irritating*? Or maybe *unprepared, uninformed, hesitant,* and *uncertain*? Would they perceive you as *rambling, boring, and windy?*

None of these words describes people you'd like to deal with. So if any of them describes you, be assured that you won't win a popularity poll with the people you call on. If you're fortunate enough to be invited in, you're unlikely to be invited back.

You're positioned for maximum selling power only when people like you, when they accept you as a competent and reliable professional, and when they know they are important to you. When prospects hear your name, they should think of words such as *friendly, knowledgeable, confident, helpful, honest,* and *considerate.* Those are the words that describe a professional.

People don't want to deal with someone who forces them to stay on guard at all times. They don't want salespeople who try to manipulate them into buying something they neither need nor want. Everything you do and say must convince your customers and prospects that they matter to you as persons, not just as buyers. You're not just out to make a buck off them; you're there to provide something of value to them.

Therefore, as a professional salesperson, you do everything you can to identify their real needs and interests.

Everyone in business has a "worry list"—a stack of problems that nag them daily and drain their creative energies. Professional salespeople try to identify the things on their prospects' worry lists. Then, they use all their professional expertise to remove the most pressing items from those lists. That's selling savvy.

(2) *"Do my prospects trust me?"*

The selling situation can get very tense. You can reduce that tension by building a strong bond between you and your prospect. Trust is the best bonding agent and the best tension-reducer. Without trust, it would be difficult to build a long-term relationship with a customer.

Impeccable integrity, total honesty, and good character are vital ingredients for positioning yourself as a trustworthy salesperson.

(3) *"Do people respect me?"*

Do they value your opinions on issues that matter to them? Your only power over your prospects is your persuasive power, and you achieve that only by convincing them that you know what you're talking about.

But as critical as all those factors are, they are only the foundation for positioning yourself for maximum selling impact. Once your prospects trust you and respect you, you still have to convince them of the importance of your message.

Remember, we listen to those people who we are convinced have something important to say to us. In fact, the more important we perceive the messenger to be, the more intently we listen to the message.

Selling savvy is knowing how to make everything you have to say of prime importance to one prospect at a time. It's knowing how to make people sit up and take notice when you speak.

Power positioning is presenting yourself to the right person, at the right time and place, in the right way, with the right message. If you can do that all day long, every day, you will be incredibly successful in sales.

Actually, what separates the real pros from the amateurs in this business of selling is their ability to make whatever they are selling of vital importance to every prospective customer.

Such positioning is not something you can achieve quickly, or once for all time. It's a continuous process of discovering new ways to take charge of the way your customers and prospects see you.

TEN EFFECTIVE STRATEGIES FOR POSITIONING

The better you plan your strategy for positioning yourself, the more successful your efforts are going to be. There are, in fact, ten crucial factors to consider as you think through your own positioning strategies and tactics. Let's look closely at each one.

(1) *Position yourself first in your own mind.*

The way you see yourself will shape the way others see you. The way you think about yourself determines the way you do everything. It affects the way you prospect, the way you interview, the way you present, the way you close, the way you follow up, and the way you manage your time. It shapes everything you do. As a result, people will see you the way you perceive yourself. If you perceive yourself as successful, others tend to perceive you as successful. If you perceive yourself as mediocre, others tend to perceive you as being mediocre.

Be Proud of Your Profession

Let me make a suggestion to you that can revolutionize your effectiveness in selling: Take a good look at the way you see yourself as a salesperson. Are you proud of your profession? Do you see yourself as a highly skilled, very competent professional person? Do you look upon yourself as a valuable resource for your company and your customers?

You can get some helpful clues about the way you see yourself by the way you respond to certain situations.

For example, how do you answer when someone at a party says, "What kind of work do you do?" Do you look embarrassed and answer with a vague "Oh, I'm in real estate" or "I'm in the automobile business"? Or do you look the person straight in the eyes and say proudly, "I'm a salesperson"?

People with selling savvy are convinced that their profession is one of the most honorable and worthy careers they could ever pursue. They know that all the factories and service organizations they represent would soon go out of business if all their salespeople quit selling. What's more, all their customers would be left without the information they need to make intelligent buying decisions.

Private Enterprise Depends on You

It is no exaggeration to say that the whole private-enterprise system would never have come into being were it not for the salespeople who support all the other functions of business.

We can hold our heads high because, as salespeople, we provide services that are absolutely essential to our society.

Remember: It's only when you believe totally in what you're doing that you can make anyone else believe in it.

So positioning starts first in your own mind. It is only when you are convinced that you are a valuable and capable person, giving value for value, that you can even begin to consider positioning yourself with your customers.

(2) *Position yourself with your attitude toward life, work, and other people.*

Some people walk into a room and say, "Here I am!" Savvy salespeople walk into a room and say, "Ah, there you are!"

For salespeople, the difference is whether you're self-centered or client-centered; whether you're ego-driven or value-driven.

Your attitude toward your customers and prospects will always show up in the way you treat people. And more than any other single factor, the way you treat others will determine the way they respond to you.

Make Your Prospect the Center of Attention

If, for example, you make yourself the center of attention in a sales interview, your prospect will resist all your efforts to move forward with the selling process. But if you make the prospect the center of attention, the barriers will come down and the prospect will move right along with you.

There's another side to having the right attitude for selling. It's maintaining a truly professional relationship with customers.

Guests or Servants?

Some salespeople think of themselves as guests, to be served by their customers. Others think of themselves as servants to be walked upon by their customers.

But the real pros in this business think of themselves as valuable resource people who help their customers get whatever they want and need out of life.

Suppose You're the Doctor

Let's look again at the way you feel when you go to a doctor. You don't want a doctor to treat you as if you were a nobody—especially if you're in severe pain.

On the other hand, you don't want the doctor simply to agree to everything you want to do.

You want the doctor to treat you with the dignity and consideration you deserve, and to command the respect that is due to a person of such expertise and competence.

In other words, you don't expect to become the center of the doctor's life, but you do expect to be treated with empathy, concern, and human courtesy.

Your customers expect the same kind of positive and professional attitude from you.

Don't be fooled into believing that you can fake a healthy attitude toward prospects. Your customers and prospects can sense the way you feel about them. Your attitude will show up in everything you do.

So if you really want to position yourself for success, cultivate the right professional attitude toward every prospect you call on.

(3) *Position yourself with your appearance.*

First impressions get set in stone very quickly. And like it or not, the way you look is the most important factor in shaping those first and lasting impressions.

If you doubt the importance of good appearance, reflect upon your own reactions to people you meet. Don't you pay more attention to people who look important than you do to people who look sloppy? Your prospects do, too. They judge your importance by the way you look.

The key is always to dress well enough to fit in with the top people you're calling on, yet never to blend in with the wallpaper. Think of your clothes as the way you package yourself.

Always dress in a way that creates the maximum positive impact on the people you want most to impress—your customers.

(4) *Position yourself with your actions.*

Your prospects determine your importance, your intentions, your reliability—and many other critical factors—by watching everything you do.

Suppose you pop in unannounced for a long visit with an extremely busy executive. What message does that convey to your prospect? It's like wearing a label that says, "pest."

Walking in with a bulging sales kit under each arm and handing out advertising gimmicks to everyone you meet is like boasting that you're a peddler.

Always think through everything you do, and the way you do it, to make sure it creates precisely the impression you want to make.

(5) *Position yourself with your words.*

Every word you say positions you either as a person to be considered important or as an intruder to be dismissed as quickly as possible.

For example, if you say, "I was in the neighborhood and thought I'd drop in," what does that say about the importance of your message? It says to the prospect, "What I have to say wasn't important enough to make a special trip to see you, but since I happened to be nearby anyway I figured I could spare you the time."

What does it say about your attitude toward the prospect? If you drop by only when you happen to be in the neighborhood, you must not regard this prospect as very valuable or important.

This positions you, in the eyes of the prospect, as a person of little importance—a person who drops in casually and haphazardly when the mood strikes. You certainly won't be perceived as a competent professional with a vital mission.

Suppose you say to your prospect, "You can't pass up a deal like this." Your prospect will see that as a presumptuous challenge and will be on guard immediately. You're saying, in effect, "Just try to stop me from making this sale," and the prospect, properly challenged, will instinctively try to stop you.

Later in this book, I'll share with you some powerful selling words that can help you create precisely the right impression. A strong selling vocabulary can make you a very persuasive salesperson.

(6) *Position yourself with your focus.*

The most pressing question on your prospect's mind is always, "What's in this for me?"

Busy people want to talk with salespeople who understand their problems and can help them find solutions. They buy for their reasons—not for yours.

When you're all caught up in your own problems and concerns, prospects can sense it, and they don't want to waste time with you.

The real pros in selling position themselves as consultants and business partners to their clients. They always keep the focus precisely where it belongs—on the customer, not on themselves or their products.

(7) *Position yourself with your presentation.*

The way you go about setting up and making your presentation says a lot to prospects about how important it is to listen to you.

If your presentation is poorly prepared, it says that you don't take it seriously, so why should they?

On the other hand, if it is too slick and relies too much on memorized phrases, it comes across as canned; it sounds insincere. The key is to practice it enough that you can give a structured presentation in a spontaneous way.

It also helps to know your material well enough that you can custom-tailor each presentation to fit each prospect's needs and concerns. The more personable and professional your presentation is, the more attention you can expect to receive.

(8) *Position yourself by the way you handle objections.*

This factor is especially crucial. Amateurs see objections as excuses for not buying or as invitations to do battle. But real pros recognize that objections show a prospect's legitimate concerns. They pinpoint the issues that must be cleared up before the prospect will make a decision to buy.

Take a close look at the way your objection-handling techniques position you in the minds of your prospects. Do you challenge your prospects when they raise objections? Or do you handle their concerns in a friendly manner, by precisely identifying the main issue that is stopping the person from buying?

(9) *Position yourself by the way you close the sale.*

The way you ask for an order can position you as a professional salesperson with a bona fide offer—an offer that provides value for the customer's money. Or it can make you look like an amateur trying to get a prospect to do you a favor.

The difference is tremendous.

Only when you've mastered the skills of closing can you close with confidence. And only when you tailor each close to fit the personality of your prospect can you position yourself as a professional.

(10) *Position yourself by the way you follow up.*

One of the most vital factors in positioning yourself as a professional salesperson is what you do once a sale has been made. If you take your signed order and make a mad dash for the door, then avoid any further contact with that customer until you want to make another sale, don't be surprised if customers start avoiding you.

Professional selling involves developing a long-term, mutually beneficial relationship with every customer you sell. It's turning one-time customers into clients who view you as a valuable resource in your area of expertise.

Your image as a professional is at least as vital to your success as is the image your company projects. It's what people think about you that determines how openly they will receive you and how attentively they will listen to what you have to say.

Positioning Yourself as a Selling Professional

What really counts in the selling game is not what you know or believe, but what your prospects think and feel.

You make them believe in you by positioning yourself as a professional—a salesperson with plenty of selling savvy.

CHECK YOUR SELLING SAVVY

I. What is "positioning"?

    _____

    _____

    _____

II. What three questions can help you determine how you're positioned for access to executive decision makers?

    (1) _____

    (2) _____

    (3) _____

III. List ten effective strategies for positioning:

    (1) _____

    (2) _____

    (3) _____

    (4) _____

    (5) _____

    (6) _____

(7) _____

(8) _____

(9) _____

(10) _____

Focusing Helps You Hit the Sales Bull's Eye

In the selling profession, it isn't hard to tell who's good and who isn't. All you have to do is look at the bottom line. Good salespeople make lots of profitable sales. Poor salespeople make few sales. When it comes to selling, the bottom line is always the bottom line. In no other profession is success so readily measurable.

You don't get paid for making sales calls. You don't get paid for making good presentations, or even for using powerful closing techniques.

Your income is always based on one criterion: your effectiveness at making sales.

Pick Your Targets and Aim

Savvy salespeople think of selling as aiming for and hitting a series of carefully chosen targets.

Of course, the one major target all salespeople aim for is making sales. They keep their eyes on their annual sales goals. But successful salespeople know that they can make sales and sales goals only when they hit all the smaller targets along the way.

Success in any business comes only when you have a clear and effective selling strategy, and when you execute that strategy all day, every day. You can be successful only when you consistently target all your sales efforts.

Selling has two critical dimensions—a macro dimension and a micro dimension. Success comes to us only when we master both of those dimensions.

THE MACRO DIMENSION

Mastering the macro dimension of selling means keeping the big picture clearly in focus at all times. It includes such strategies as:

- Understanding your business and your customers.
- Constantly sharpening your selling skills.
- Learning to shorten the sales cycle.
- Regularly refocusing your overall sales goals and strategies.

THE MICRO DIMENSION

Mastering the micro dimension of selling means staying in complete control of every minute detail of each selling situation. It's paying attention to everything that must happen if you are to close each sale.

Controlling the micro dimension of selling includes such tactics as:

- Watching and responding to every move the customer makes and staying alert to anything in the selling environment that might have an impact on the sale.
- Bringing every event in the selling process to a satisfactory closure.
- Following up on every detail involved in executing the sale.

I've led thousands of sales seminars over many years, and I've met many salespeople who were reasonably good at operating in one of those dimensions. They had mastered either the macro or the micro dimension.

But salespeople who master both the macro and the micro dimensions are extremely rare—and extremely successful. They are truly effective salespeople. They possess selling savvy.

Since we're going to look very closely at the micro dimension of selling in the chapters that follow, let's zero in for now on the macro dimension—the big picture.

Find Your Focus

Targeting the big picture in selling means bringing your goals, objectives, and strategies clearly into focus. It means knowing precisely what you want to achieve, deciding exactly how you will go about it, and doing everything that is necessary to make it happen.

Truly successful salespeople are effective because they make solid commitments to targeting. They set goals for total sales volume, for prospecting, for each sales interview, and for each presentation. They target the way they close, the way they follow up sales calls, and the way they manage their time.

They think of their goals as bull's eyes, and they focus everything they do on hitting their targets. That's why they make sales, not excuses.

If you're dissatisfied with your effectiveness and want to sell smart, you must make a solid commitment to targeting. Then, as you clarify your targets, you must focus all your abilities on consistently hitting those targets.

How do you do that?

COMMIT TO GOALS

A commitment to targeting begins with setting practical, realistic, results-oriented goals.

Here are ten good reasons why goals can make you more successful at selling:

(1) *Goals give you something to work for.*

A good set of goals will give purpose and direction to your life. When you have a purpose to work toward, it gives direction to all your efforts. When you are driven by a strong purpose, you have a strong motivation to work harder and look for more effective ways to do things.

(2) *Goals keep you from procrastinating.*

When you have a set objective, you don't want to put things off. You know that every task you accomplish moves you closer to your goal.

(3) *Goals build enthusiasm.*

Goals give you something to get excited about. When you have a set of goals, you know what you want, and you know what you are going to do to get it.

(4) *Goals help you be specific with all the other people who want to assist you along the way.*

If you ask people, in a general way, to do something "when you get around to it," it may be a long time, if ever, before they get around to it. But when you ask that specific things be done by a specific time, you'll see things get done.

(5) *Goals help you save time.*

Goals will help you save time for you, your clients, and everyone else in your life. They almost force you to get organized, so you can accomplish everything you set out to do.

(6) *Goals help you make money.*

They'll also save you money. Targeting helps you invest all your resources in ways that use them to their greatest potential.

(7) *Goals help you focus on what's important instead of what's urgent.*

There's a marked difference between what's urgent and what's important. An important task is something that moves you toward your goal. An urgent task may not be very important in the long run, but it demands immediate attention.

If the roof is leaking and water is dripping on your valuable armoire, the urgent task is to move the furniture. Moving the armoire doesn't solve your problem; it doesn't move you toward your goal of a weather-tight house. But if you don't move it, serious consequences occur.

Yet, in the long run, the important task is to fix the roof.

The difference is perhaps best illustrated by the case of the man who says he can't drain the swamp because he's up to his waist in alligators. The urgent task is fighting off the alligators. The important task is draining the swamp.

A major difference between amateur and professional salespeople is their ability to focus on important tasks by minimizing urgent tasks. You minimize urgent tasks by spotting problems while they're still minor and easily remedied, and taking care of them at once. Replacing a loose shingle on the roof when you first spot it may prevent the leak that threatens to ruin your antique armoire. Taking care of a minor service problem as soon as a customer calls it to your attention may prevent major problems down the road, and prevent you from losing a major account.

If you keep in perspective what's really important, you won't spend all your time doing what seems urgent.

(8) *Goals give you a standard against which you can measure your effectiveness.*

If you have a set of measurable goals, you can tell at any given moment how well you are doing. You'll know whether you're moving toward success or wandering aimlessly, accepting whatever comes your way.

When you achieve each goal, you can reward yourself. When you fail to reach a goal, you can analyze the reasons for the failure and use that knowledge to build toward your next success.

(9) *Goals provide an excellent reference point for setting new targets.*

As you accomplish one goal, it's easier to use that achievement as the reference point for setting a new target.

If you meet your goal of a 10% increase over last year's volume, you have a new standard by which to measure success. If your volume is actually up by 15%, perhaps you'll want to aim higher than 10% next year. If you aimed for 25% and achieved only 12%, perhaps you should consider whether your high target is realistic. A 15% goal may be more appropriate. If you have goals, you know whether you're moving close to your target. Without goals, you're shooting in the dark.

(10) *Goals help you take advantage of momentum.*

Every goal you reach gives you an energizing sense of accomplishment. "Nothing succeeds like success" is a cliché, but like most clichés, it's true.

Your motivation flows from your subconscious mind. If it believes you're a success, it will cause you to act like a success. It will direct you in a pattern of behavior that will lead to achievement.

How do you make your subconscious mind believe that you're a big success?

By feeding it a steady diet of small successes. Your subconscious mind can't tell the difference between little successes and big successes. So set some achievable goals in little endeavors, and go after them. Once you've achieved them, pause to congratulate yourself. Subconsciously, you'll be saying, "Hey, I'm successful." And you'll be far more likely to be successful in the next big project you undertake. Each success becomes a springboard to the next success.

Draw Lessons From the Successful

Some of the best advice I ever received was this: "If you would be successful, study the lives of successful people, figure out the systems that made them successful and adapt them to your own life."

If you examine the lives of great people, you'll discover that they had one thing in common: They knew where they were going. They were all aiming at targets.

Goals help you to concentrate all your energies and resources in a specific direction. They help you focus the full power of your abilities toward increased effectiveness. And that's a lot of power.

FOCUS ON GOALS THAT WORK

But selling savvy requires more than setting goals. About 98% of all salespeople believe in setting goals, and most of them think they are doing a fairly good job of it. But setting goals doesn't land the commission. Achieving the goals is what puts money in the account.

Most salespeople don't know how to focus their energies toward a target. Without that focus, achieving the goals becomes increasingly difficult.

So let's look at some tested and proven ways to focus all your power, energy, and talents effectively on goals that will work for you.

Remember: Targets have meaning only when they produce tangible results in the real world of selling. Seven guidelines have helped me achieve results, and they'll help you set targets you can hit—goals you can reach:

(1) *Set goals that are consistent with your purpose in life.*

One way to determine your purpose in life is to write down what you want most out of life. You might be surprised at what you discover about yourself.

For example, many people say that what they want most is to become extremely wealthy. Yet, if you were to suggest that they link up with a drug cartel, you'd quickly learn that money is not the most important thing in their lives.

If you don't believe in your goals—if they are not consistent with your purpose in life—you are destined to fail. You won't be committed to those goals.

(2) *Set goals that you can get excited about.*

It won't help you to pursue goals that excite your boss, your neighbor or your in-laws. It's your own subconscious, not theirs, that gives you the motivation and direction to succeed.

Many salespeople fall short of their quotas because they're goals somebody else has set for them. When you're not personally involved in setting the goals, you find it hard to get very excited about them.

What is it that excites you? A new home? A vacation in the Bahamas? A promotion?

The great thing about selling is that you can write your own ticket. You can make enough money to turn your dreams into realities. It's all up to you.

You will be amazed at how much more effective you will become if you find something that you can become enthusiastic about and structure your goals around that dream.

(3) *Set goals that meet your needs as a total person.*

Don't set goals for yourself only as a salesperson and leave no room for other vital areas of your life. It's possible to maintain a well-balanced life and still have plenty of time to be very successful at selling.

Some of the most successful salespeople I know have very good family relationships. They are thoroughly committed to their churches, and many are very active in their communities. In addition, they still have time to pursue hobbies.

Salespeople such as these have learned the value of setting goals in all areas of their lives.

(4) *Set goals that are high enough to deserve your very best, but not so high that they are unreachable.*

"Ah, but a man's reach should exceed his grasp, or what's a heaven for?" wrote Robert Browning, the 19th century English poet.

If you follow Browning's philosophy, you're going to need a heaven, because your earthly life is going to be full of frustration. Achieving your goals is one of the most enriching experiences of life.

Individual goals are very personal things, and only you can decide what goals are high enough for you. A good goal will make you stretch, but it won't cause you to break.

Building toward success is like building muscles. The muscles must be stretched or they won't grow. You can lift a feather pillow all day long and it won't build your biceps. To do that, you have to pump iron.

You can pursue easy goals all year long and they won't stretch you. Your performance won't get better, because you're not challenging yourself to get better.

You won't build muscles either by trying to lift a freight car off the tracks. To do you any good, the weight must be liftable.

It's the same way with your personal goals. They must be goals that you can achieve if you put enough effort into them.

At first, it may be a matter of guessing at what is beyond your grasp, and what is too easily gained. But after some experience at setting and reaching goals, you will learn what goals are appropriate for you.

(5) *Set goals that are specific and measurable.*

Vague goals are of little use. It won't do you much good if your goal this year is to "make enough money to live comfortably."

What does it mean to "live comfortably"? How much money does it take?

You need to set a specific target: "My goal is to sell 1,000 units this year," "My goal is $65,000 in commissions by the end of the year," or "My goal is to increase my sales volume by 10% over last year's volume."

With specific goals such as these, you'll know when you've reached them. You'll also be able to calculate your progress toward reaching them.

If your annual goal is 1,000 units, you know you'll have to sell about 85 units a month to be safely on track. If you're aiming for 85 units a month, you know you must average 20 to 25 a week to reach your target.

It's important that you perceive yourself as making progress, even if it's in small increments. Remember the adage: "A yard is hard, but an inch is a cinch." A 100% increase in sales may sound like an impossible target. But a 10% increase may be well within the range of possibility. Meet your 10% goal each year for ten years and what do you have? A 100% increase.

If you stack 36 books one on top of the other, it looks like a hopeless stack of reading. But if you aim toward reading three books a month, you'll finish all 36 in a year. And you'll probably do more reading than will the person whose target is "to read everything I can get my hands on."

Unclear goals are as useless as no goals at all. Make them measurable, make them specific, and make them challenging but achievable.

(6) *Write down your goals.*

An Eastern proverb tells us that "The palest ink is better than the most remarkable memory."

People who have been selling for years know that until they receive the signed order, they have no sale. Before you have a sale, you have to get the customer's commitment to buy.

It's the same way with goals. A goal is a promise—a commitment you make to yourself and to other people who matter to you.

Take your goals seriously, just as you would a contract. You might even want to draw them up as a contract with yourself. Then, date it and sign it.

Once you have written your goals, keep them where you can read them often. That'll help you keep them clearly in focus.

(7) *Set a deadline for each goal.*

Deadlines motivate you to work consistently toward reaching your goals.

If you say, "I'm going to do that someday," you're falling into a common trap. "Someday" is a rough synonym for "never."

Commit to Targeting

Truly successful salespeople are effective because they make solid commitments to targeting. They set goals for total sales volume, for prospecting, for each sales interview, and for each presentation. They target the way they close, the way they follow up sales calls, and the way they manage their time.

They think of their goals as bull's eyes, and they focus everything they do on hitting their targets. That's why they make sales, not excuses.

If you're dissatisfied with your effectiveness and want to sell smart, you must make a solid commitment to targeting. Then, as you clarify your targets, you must focus all your abilities on consistently hitting those targets.

Three Categories of Goals

One good way to set realistic deadlines is to divide your goals into three categories—long-range, intermediate-range, and immediate.

Long-range targets are your overall goals for the next five to ten years. A long-range goal for a salesperson might be "to become regional sales manager for the company."

Intermediate-range targets involve smaller goals, which are steps on your path toward your long-range goals. For example, an intermediate goal that would lead to the long-range goal of becoming a sales manager could be "to increase my sales by 20% each year."

Intermediate-range goals can usually be covered in a year or two.

Immediate goals are the day-to-day objectives that will lead you step-by-step to your long-range goals. An immediate goal to help you toward that 20% goal might be "to increase the number of weekly cold calls by 50%."

This type of goal can cover one to six months.

Setting effective targets is the best way to increase your effectiveness as a salesperson. If you use the seven guidelines I've suggested, you'll find it simple to do—and very helpful.

Develop Strategies for Reaching Your Goals

But setting goals is only one-third of the requirement for getting the macro dimension of selling in clear focus. The next step is to develop the strategies for reaching those goals.

Most salespeople spend 80% of their time on the tasks that produce only 20% of their sales. That's why most salespeople aren't successful.

Unsuccessful salespeople invest most of their time and effort on support work—shuffling papers and processing orders. Then, they wonder why they have so little time for prospecting, presentations, and follow-up—activities that produce most of their income.

Don't Stay Busy at the Wrong Things

Why is it so easy to get caught in that trap?

It's because they don't really understand what they have to do to reach their goals. They have no plans—no strategies for success.

Notice that I didn't say they were lazy. Some of the least successful salespeople I've ever met have been some of the hardest workers. They just stay busy doing the wrong things.

The problem is clear: They haven't learned the secret of doing the right things—the things that will bring in more and bigger sales.

For example, a survey done by the New York Marketing Executives Association revealed that the typical salesperson spends fewer than three hours each day with prospects. The average first sales call of the day is made after 11 a.m. It's not that the salespeople are lazy. It's just that they have no strategy for success.

They're caught up in the activity syndrome. A good strategy for increasing your sales by 20% would be to make your first sales call by 8 a.m. every day. That way, you can get a three-hour jump on most of your competitors.

If you want to increase your effectiveness, you simply must develop a workable strategy for reaching each goal.

Your goals are only as productive as your strategies for reaching them. The best idea is useless without a plan to make it work.

So that's two-thirds of the targeting formula—setting high but reachable goals, and creating workable strategies to reach them.

Execute Your Strategies

But even the best ideas and plans are useless unless you add the third ingredient: execution.

In selling, more than in any other profession, nothing happens until you make it happen. You have to execute your plans.

Have you ever noticed the recorded times of Olympic races? Most of the races are won by a few hundredths of a second, even though the event might last for more than an hour.

The winners are usually not superhuman; they are just a little bit better than their competition. But that slight edge is the secret to their success.

Some of those athletes train for years. They practice endlessly for an event that may take only a few minutes. And then they win by only a slim margin.

If you study their training programs, you'll find that all of them have made a practice of setting goals. They have developed solid strategies for reaching their goals. Then, on the field of competition, they've given it everything they had.

They are committed. And they are dedicated to reaching their goals.

Join the Top 5%

For every gold-medal winner, there are thousands of young people who started out to reach that goal. But somewhere along the way, they lost their focus on their goals. They lost their focus on their strategies. Or they simply failed to execute.

Setting realistic goals and strategies, then giving everything you've got to meet those goals, provides the winner's competitive edge.

Salespeople who consistently set their next goals somewhat above their last achievements, and who consider all their targets as vitally important, become increasingly effective.

The professional with selling savvy understands the value of goals and strategies. And, for that reason, you'll find that truly professional salespeople are to be found in the top 5% of all salespeople.

If you want to join the ranks of the most successful, put your selling savvy into action, and start targeting for success.

Then, give everything you've got to become all you want to be.

CHECK YOUR SELLING SAVVY

I. Name four strategies in the macro dimension of selling:

    (1) _____

    (2) _____

    (3) _____

    (4) _____

II. Name three strategies in the micro dimension of selling:

    (1) _____

    (2) _____

    (3) _____

III. List seven guidelines for focusing effectively on goals:

(1) _____

(2) _____

(3) _____

(4) _____

(5) _____

(6) _____

(7) _____

The Power in the Seven *P*'s of Selling

I have a friend, a sales manager in my hometown of High Point, North Carolina, who calls his people together every Monday morning and tells them:

"Now, we all know that many people can talk in glowing terms about products or services. Even amateurs can stage interesting presentations. Some can even make strong cases to prospects for buying their products."

"But the real pros in the selling world are those who can persuade plenty of prospects to act—to make buying decisions and follow through with them."

My friend is on to the *7-P* factor in selling: your *p*ower to *p*ersuade *p*lenty of *p*rospects to *p*urchase your *p*roducts at a *p*rofit to you. Your success as a salesperson depends, ultimately, on your ability to put these seven *P*'s into practice.

PERSISTENCE WITHOUT PRESSURE

My High Point friend would tack another *P* onto that list: *p*ersistence, or *p*erseverance.

I'll accept his recommendation, with one word of caution: Your *p*ersistence should not turn into *p*ressure.

Professional selling is not manipulating people into buying things they don't want or need. It's not a game in which you apply pressure until the prospect gives in.

And success in selling doesn't mean that you have to abandon all of your principles and personal integrity just to get people to buy. In fact, it calls for putting your principles and personal integrity into practice on behalf of your company and your customers.

Your role as a salesperson is to influence prospects to buy. That involves a lot more than just being nice to them. To be successful, you must be able to persuade them to buy without pressuring them.

Patience Builds Relationships

Persistence calls for another *P—p*atience. The professional salesperson patiently cultivates prospects, making as many calls as necessary to learn the prospect's needs and finding a way to satisfy those needs.

Professional salespeople don't think in terms of individual sales. They think in terms of long-term relationships. It's these relationships that pay off in repeat business.

Some years ago, an organization called Sales and Marketing Executives conducted a survey to determine the number of times salespeople have to call on an individual prospect to make a sale. It found that more than 80% of all sales require at least five calls. Only 2% are closed on the first call. About 3% require two calls, 4% require three, and 10% require four. The impatient salesperson who quits after the first or second call will rarely reach pay dirt.

Sales Are Like Touchdowns

Making sales is like scoring touchdowns in football. The quarterback who tries to score a touchdown on every play will rarely put points on the board. The professional quarterback knows that he has to move his team downfield a few yards on every play. He tries to put those few yards together for a succession of first downs that keep him in possession of the ball. On each play, he analyzes the other team's defense and devises his strategy for the next play. Each play builds upon the previous play until at last he is within striking distance and can go for the end zone.

Similarly, professional salespeople have the patience to make repeated calls, each one moving them systematically toward a sale. Like a quarterback analyzing the opposing defense, they analyze their prospects. But unlike the quarterback, they're not out to defeat the prospects. They're out to learn about the prospects, find out about their needs and problems, and look for ways to make life more pleasant and business more profitable for them.

One Step at a Time

So if you're a professional salesperson, you do your homework. Your aim on each call is to move the prospect another step closer to the sale. Find out what information you need to take that step, and be sure you have it when you make the call. Devise a strategy for each call based on where you were on your last call. Don't make every call a cold call. Remember that only about eight sales are made for every 100 cold calls. Work toward making every call warmer than the one before until you get that sale.

Selling at a Profit

It isn't enough to help your prospects—to offer them products or services that can improve the quality of their lives or add to the ease and profitability of doing business. You also want them to buy your products at a profit to you and to the company you work for. If your company doesn't make a profit, it can't continue to invest in future growth and development.

A successful sale is one that makes both the seller and the buyer better off than they were before the sale. When both sides win, then each side has a stronger reason to do business with the other in the future. That's why the win/win approach is the approach of choice for all successful salespeople.

Some Sales Aren't Worth It

Professional salespeople know that some sales are not worth the time, effort, and expense to get them. They think not only of the gross proceeds from a sale but also of the net. How much time and effort did it take to make the sale? What kind of commitment did you have to make to get it, and what will that commitment cost in the future? What kind of price concessions did you have to make? What are the prospects for cross-selling in the future?

Amateur salespeople often look upon a sale as an end unto itself. The professionals know that the ultimate end is a profitable relationship. Amateur salespeople often cut their prices to the bone to make a sale. Professionals know that price is rarely the decisive factor in a sale. Prospects are looking for value, and they look for it not only in the product itself but also in the salesperson and the company the salesperson represents.

MAKE YOURSELF VALUABLE

One of the things that makes you a professional salesperson is your ability to make yourself valuable to the customer—to render a service for which people are willing to pay.

If you want to make a successful sale, don't cut prices; build value. If you build enough value, your prospect will buy and your company will make a profit.

We'll elaborate on that in a future chapter, but for the moment, let's focus on ways to add power to your persuasion without turning it into pressure. That's a crucial ingredient in selling savvy.

Persuasion With Power

One of the most important factors distinguishing successful people from mediocrities is their ability to persuade with power. They are able to move people to action.

That doesn't mean that all successful people come roaring into action the way General Patton roared into Germany. Many of them are like Omar Bradley, the "soldier's general"—quiet, thoughtful, and low-key people who get their way because people admire them, respect them, and trust their judgments.

Do good salespeople put a lot of pressure on their prospects? Are they aggressive and insensitive? Are they of the type that could win an argument with a signpost?

Not today's successful salespeople; not in today's sales environment.

Some of the most successful salespeople I know are laid-back, easygoing people. They are very considerate of their prospective clients. They know that prospects are their bread and butter—and their cake and ice cream, too.

They are professionals who use persuasion to influence their clients to buy. They know that the best prospect for future sales is a happy customer. They sell to sell again.

Do you want to boost your selling power? Then, add power to your persuasion.

Let me give it to you in the form of a guarantee: If you learn enough from this chapter to increase your persuasive power by 10%, then you can increase your sales by at least 10%.

TEN POINTERS FOR POWER PERSUASION

But how can you add power to your persuasion? How can you become more effective at persuading your customers to buy?

Let's look at the way the skilled professionals put power into their ability to persuade.

Let me share with you ten secrets I've learned from some of the most persuasive salespeople in America—ten ways to add power to your persuasion. I call them the ten *P*'s of persuasion.

(1) *Be positive.*

One of the most successful insurance salesmen in America is a country fellow from South Georgia, who says, "You can no more sell something you don't believe in, than you can come back from some place you ain't been."

Successful salespeople are positive people.

They have positive mental attitudes about themselves, the companies they represent, the products or services they're selling, the prospects they're attempting to persuade, and the country they live in. They're positive about everything.

Enthusiasm is contagious. When you're excited about life and the work you're doing, you can persuade with power, because you can get other people excited.

(2) *Prospect.*

Successful salespeople have learned to direct their persuasive power toward people who have the resources to buy and have good reasons to buy what they are selling.

It's easy to spot amateurs at selling. They waste time by trying to persuade people who have no need or no desire to buy, or people who have no authority or no money to buy.

Professional salespeople concentrate on people who can buy. Sometimes, a secretary says, "Tell me what you are selling, and I'll tell Ms. Jones. If she's interested, she'll call you." You won't find real pros spilling their story to that secretary. The skilled persuader directs all efforts toward getting an appointment with Ms. Jones.

Professional salespeople pinpoint prospects who are likely to provide long-term profitability. They analyze the possibilities for cross-selling. They know that it takes an average of three calls to cross-sell an existing customer but seven to sell to a new customer.

Use Referrals Like a Pro

They also know the value of referrals. They know that referral calls are about 3 1/2 times as productive as cold calls. But they also know that there's a professional's way and an amateur's way to ask for referrals.

The amateur will ask a friend or customer, "How about giving me the names of some of your friends who might be interested in my product."

When you ask for a referral that way, you'll get the first few names that pop into the person's head. Maybe they'll need your product; maybe they won't. Maybe they can afford it; maybe they can't. Maybe they'll be in position to make the decision; maybe they won't.

Professional salespeople specify the criteria for the kind of prospects they're seeking: "Whom do you know who runs an office with 10 or 15 employees who could make use of computer networking?"

You may get fewer names with that kind of question, but they'll be the names of people who are most likely to need your equipment or services and to be in a position to buy.

If you use the professional's approach, you'll be chasing fewer unproductive calls and focusing more of your efforts on the people who need and want what you're selling.

Professional salespeople know who their best customers are, and put the 80/20 rule to work for them. They spend most of their time with the 20 percent of their customers who provide 80% of their profits.

In short, the powerful persuader targets all efforts at the person who has the resources, the motivation, and the authority to buy, and the potential for profitable repeat sales.

(3) *Prepare.*

Red Motley, who started *Parade* magazine, said that the average salesperson will work like crazy to get an appointment, then blow the opportunity with a poor presentation after the decision maker has agreed to the interview.

You don't make sales to busy people by rambling on for 40 minutes about features and benefits. Usually, after such disjointed presentations, neither the salesperson nor the prospect can summarize what's just been said.

Amateurs waste golden opportunities simply because they either don't prepare or don't prepare well enough.

Professional salespeople always do their homework. They know that the better they're prepared, the more persuasive they'll be when they walk in to make a presentation.

They research to find out everything they need to know about the prospect. They plan what they will show and what they will say. And they practice, practice, practice.

If you want to talk about the Super Bowl, become a sportcaster. If you want to talk about the weather, become a meteorologist.

But if you want to become a powerful persuader, find out what your prospects stay up at night worrying about.

Then, prepare your presentations to show precisely how you can solve each prospect's problem. Plan precisely what you will do for each presentation. Then, do it. Proper preparation prevents poor performance.

Go in Informed

Professional salespeople rarely go into a prospect's office and say "Tell me about your business." They've already informed themselves about the business. The sharp salesperson will know the correct name of the company, who owns it, who its top executives are, how long it has been in business, how many employees it has, and what its annual sales are.

The well-prepared salesperson will also know the company's chief products, its chief customers, and its chief suppliers.

Much of this information can be obtained by telephone well in advance of a sales call. Some of it can be obtained from publications, and some from referrals and networking. Professional salespeople find and cultivate sources of information.

(4) *Perform.*

Amateur salespeople complain furiously when they are beaten out by a competitor. How could that customer buy that overpriced, poor-quality product? He must be an idiot!

The customer was no idiot. The complainer was just outperformed by a more competitive salesperson.

Remember: People don't buy; they're sold. In fact, nothing is ever bought. Everything has to be sold. If you don't make a strong presentation, you can't persuade your prospect to buy.

Powerful persuaders are like stage actors playing to a full house. They are artists at making their presentations. They're entertaining and informative to watch and hear.

When they've finished their presentations, their customers will have the information necessary to make decisions. And those customers will be motivated to do what the salesperson is asking them to do: buy!

Do you know why many of America's most successful companies spend up to half a million dollars to make one prime-time television commercial?

Those corporations know that they have just a few seconds to capture the attention of a television audience; a few seconds to persuade viewers to buy their products.

When the tape rolls, and masses of people are watching, it's action time! That short commercial had better sell with all the persuasive power the advertisers can put into it.

How much "action time" do you have each day? Action time is the precious few minutes you have to make your sales presentation.

To succeed in this business, you have to make every second of every minute of your "action time" count.

To add power to your persuasion, add performance to your presentation. Give every presentation your best shot.

(5) *Be perceptive.*

Powerful persuaders are alert to everything that happens during a sales interview.

They are not preoccupied with personal problems, with airline schedules, or even with the next call they are going to make. They know that reaching a sales goal always begins with making the sale at hand.

Powerful persuaders tune into their prospects and look for the motivating forces in the life of each. Once they discover that motivating force, they play to the motivation.

Let's look at a simple example. If you are selling cars and you pick up the clue that luxury and performance are the features most important to a prospect, you don't lead them to your mini-vans or your sport-utility vehicles. You lead them to that plush, powerful luxury sedan that takes off like a rocket and glides like a yacht.

By being perceptive about the motivations of each prospect, the professional salesperson appeals to the "hot button"—the prospect's key reason for buying.

But the professional salesperson is also attuned to negative feedback from prospects, and is able to detect hidden reasons for their hesitance to buy.

This approach enables you to expose the problem and deal with it. You can't solve a problem until you understand what it is.

To add power to your persuasion, learn to be perceptive—to read your prospects and to discover the motivations they have to buy or not to buy.

(6) *Probe.*

Average salespeople do a lot of talking. They can give you a 30-minute speech on any subject you want to name.

That's why silence is so threatening to most salespeople. The instant a prospect pauses to take a breath, the amateur will jump in with a sales spiel, just to break the silence.

But powerful persuaders use questions to diagnose the needs and concerns of a prospect much as a skilled physician uses them to diagnose the problems of a patient.

They become masters at asking penetrating questions, and they use those questions to draw prospects into the selling process.

This business of probing is so important that we will devote an entire chapter to it later in the book.

The art of asking questions is one of the most useful tools for people who become persuasive and successful salespeople.

(7) *Personalize.*

The most powerful word in selling is *you.*

The emphasis on *you* marks the difference between manipulative and non-manipulative selling.

Manipulative selling is self-centered. It focuses on what the salesperson wants and needs.

Non-manipulative selling is client-centered. It focuses on the needs and desires of the prospect.

A person who is looking at the business proposition you are offering wants to know just one thing: What's in it for me?

For example, successful real-estate salespeople know that a house is not sold until the prospective owners take "psychological possession" of it.

They're concerned about the needs of the customers and gear everything in their presentations to that magic moment when a client stops calling it a house and starts calling it home.

If you want to add power to your persuasion, personalize every part of your presentation to meet your prospect's own personal needs and wants.

(8) *Please.*

Powerful persuaders seek to close sales by pleasing their clients. When prospects become excited about the idea of owning what you're selling, they become customers.

Professional salespeople know that they can't force their prospects to buy. Their challenge is to make them *want* to buy. So they seek to please them in so many ways that they create the desire to buy.

Different people have different motivations, and therefore you must take different routes to please them. Some people are highly competitive and motivated by the desire to win. So the professional salesperson will look for ways to make them winners. Others are socially active. They're motivated by a desire to be admired and respected among their peers. So you look for ways to make them shine and excel. Others are motivated by a desire to be of service; they yearn for a stable world in which they can enjoy the esteem of their acquaintances. Selling professionals will emphasize the way their products or services help them achieve these ends. Others are concerned more with the way things work. They want things to be practical, and they want them to be reliable and effective. With such a person, the skilled salesperson emphasizes the product.

Sell Yourself as Well as the Product

People who are strictly of a technical frame of mind will buy the right product even if they don't particularly like the salesperson. But such people are in the minority. Most people want to buy from people they like and trust, and it's up to the salesperson to build that trust and that esteem.

My friend Charles Dygert likes to tell of a roofing salesperson who actually suggested that a client buy from a competitor, even though it meant losing a $500,000 sale. The salesperson had the most expensive roofing product in its field; it was guaranteed for 30 years. But the salesperson knew that the building was old, and through questioning he learned that the customer planned to tear it down within 15 years. So the salesperson sent the customer to a roofing company that could provide a roof guaranteed for 15 years at half the cost.

Many salespeople would think that salesperson was insane. But he was thinking about long-term relationships, not individual sales. He was building trust, and it paid off. The customer promptly got on the telephone to every purchasing agent he knew and said "If you need a new roof, go to this guy. He'll tell you the truth about what you need."

The pros learn to size up individuals quickly. They can tell by the looks of an office whether they're dealing with someone whose key motivation is winning, excelling, serving, or doing things right. They look at the items on the walls and on the desks. They know that the technical perfectionist is likely to keep a neat office. They know that the service-oriented individual will have walls lined with certificates of good deeds performed. They learn to read their prospects quickly and to direct their efforts toward pleasing them and making them want to buy.

(9) *Prove.*

Salespeople with selling savvy don't make statements they can't back up with facts.

And they don't expect their clients to accept at face value everything they say. They are always prepared to prove every claim they make—to back up those claims with hard data, with test results, and with performance records.

But be sure the proof is authentic. Don't be like the mobile-home salesperson who liked to demonstrate the sturdiness of his product by slamming his fist into the walls. He knew—or thought he knew—where all the studs were, so his fist struck solid wall. But on one new model, he miscalculated the location of the studs—twice. He lost the sale and ended up with a sore fist and a product with two ugly holes in the wall.

One of the best ways to persuade by proving is to give proof statements from people who are happy with your products or services. Third-party endorsements go a long way in building credibility for your claims, and for your products.

Facts and testimonials are very persuasive. Learn to use them, and become a powerful persuader.

(10) *Persist.*

Call on good prospects as many times as it takes to sell them.

Remember that study by Sales and Marketing Executives. About 80% of sales are made on the fifth call or later. Yet, studies have shown that:

♦ 50% of America's salespeople call on a prospect one time and quit.

- 18% call on a prospect twice and give up.
- 7% call three times and call it quits.
- 5% call on a prospect four times before quitting.
- Only 20% call on a prospect five or more times before they quit.

It's that 20% who close 80% of the sales in America.

You don't have to become a dynamic personality to sell. You don't have to put pressure on people or out-talk people to sell.

The most effective thing you can do is to apply your own selling savvy to these ten ways to add strength to your persuasion.

Learn how to persuade more effectively and you will boost your selling power.

CHECK YOUR SELLING SAVVY

I. What are the seven P's of selling?

_____

_____

II. List ten pointers for power persuasion:

(1) _____

(2) _____

(3) _____

(4) _____

(5) _____

(6) _____

(7) _____

(8) _____

(9) _____

(10) _____

Good Communication Means Great Sales

If you want to sell, you have to communicate. Information has to pass between you and the prospect, and on the basis of that information, your prospect decides whether to buy or pass.

Whether the answer is sale or no sale will depend, to a great extent, on your skill in conveying information to the prospect and processing the information your prospect conveys to you. This process of conveying and receiving information is what we call communication.

Mind-to-Mind Orientation

To be a persuasive salesperson requires strong communication skills. A persuasive salesperson can sell a mediocre product better than a mediocre salesperson can sell a great product.

It's not enough to be able to talk fast and to ramble on about the features of whatever you are selling; even the amateur salespeople do that. In his book, *The 7 Habits of Highly Effective People,* author Stephen Covey lists as Habit no. 5, "Seek first to understand, and then to be understood." Professional salespeople with savvy know that their challenge is to convey the proper message and to have it understood clearly. This calls for "mind-to-mind orientation" with the customer.

Mind-to-mind orientation means that you get a clear picture of what the prospect is thinking and feeling, and in turn you convey your thoughts clearly to the prospect. The interchange of thoughts is crucial to communication. If the information is flowing only in one direction, that's not communication. The word *communication* comes from a Latin word that means "to share." If you're not sharing thoughts and ideas, you're not communicating, and you're not selling.

COMMUNICATE THROUGH DIALOGUE

That's why the skillful salesperson learns to communicate through *dialogue.* A dialogue is a conversation between two parties. If just one person is talking, that's a monologue. Dialogue, by my definition, is what happens when the reality within you makes contact with the reality within your listener, and together you move toward a common new reality.

Effective communication is:

(1) Presenting your ideas clearly, concisely, and with power.
(2) Making sure prospects understand your ideas and business proposals.
(3) Listening carefully to understand the needs and wants of prospects and to obtain feedback that may indicate misconceptions on the part of prospects.
(4) Clearing up any misconceptions a prospect may have about your products or services.
(5) Showing prospects precisely how you can serve them.

These communication skills are absolutely essential to successful selling. The most magnificent product or offer will not move clients to buy if they don't understand what you are offering and how it will benefit them.

In this chapter, you'll discover how effective communication can help you sell more successfully, and you'll learn some pointers that will enable you to sharpen your skills.

Great Communicators of the Past

When you think of great communicators in history, who's the first person that comes into your mind?

Maybe you think about Abraham Lincoln's eloquent appeal for a war-weary nation to do its utmost so that "the government of the people, by the people and for the people shall not perish from the earth."

Maybe you think of Franklin Roosevelt, who communicated hope during the darkest days of depression and war.

Maybe you think of Winston Churchill, whose dynamic speeches inspired a beleaguered Britain to endure and fight against the awesome force of Nazi Germany during World War II.

Or perhaps you remember the dramatic cadences of Martin Luther King, Jr. in his famous "I have a dream . . ." speech, which stirred the national conscience.

How did these people achieve greatness? What made them such effective leaders? Why were they able to sell their ideas so successfully?

Their chief instrument was language skillfully employed: the ability to communicate their messages to others in such a way that others were motivated to act. That ability sets the great leader apart from the mediocre crowd.

Whether you are trying to sell hope and courage to a troubled nation or attempting to sell a widget to a single consumer, the principles of communication are the same: Effective selling is effective communication.

Our goal in this chapter is to explore some tested and proven techniques that can help you boost your selling power by building your communication skills.

THE SLO METHOD OF COMMUNICATION

Three basic elements have impact on your communication. They can be organized into the SLO method of communication. The formula consists of:

- ◆ Speaking.
- ◆ Listening.
- ◆ Observing.

Everything You Do Sends a Message

You send messages to your customers in many different ways. Speaking is the most obvious way, but everything about you and everything you do sends messages. Consciously or unconsciously, you are constantly sending messages whenever you are in the presence of other people.

Your appearance, your physical motions, and your facial expressions all say something about you to your prospects. In fact, it's been said that 93% of our communication is non-verbal. Yet, many people, including those beating their brains out day after day trying to sell, pay almost no attention to these important message-senders.

If you look at the images of Winston Churchill on the newsreels of World War II, you will see a man who exuded confidence and bulldog determination. A man who went around with a beaten look on his face could not have rallied a desperate nation to come off the ropes and stand up to the mighty aggressor. A man with a mournful air about him could not have inspired his people with an offer of "blood, toil, tears and sweat." When Churchill flashed his "V for victory" sign, the British people believed him because his manner and appearance exuded confidence and defiance, and the nation reflected his optimism.

When people saw Franklin Roosevelt during the Great Depression and the epic war that followed it, they didn't see a crippled man struggling to stay on his feet, although he wore braces in the aftermath of polio. They saw a jaunty president who was eager to lead and confident that "the only thing we have to fear is fear itself."

When they saw Martin Luther King, Jr., they didn't see a wisecracking, street-talking radical, and they didn't see a shuffling, submissive wimp. They saw a dignified man, dressed conservatively and tastefully, who spoke of freedom and justice. When such a man is beaten and jailed, the national conscience recoils.

Churchill, Roosevelt, Lincoln, and King spoke not only with words but also with their attitudes and their appearances. They knew that they were constantly on stage, and they saw to it that the images they projected reinforced the verbal messages they were sending.

One of the most important steps in effective communication, if you want to be a professional salesperson, is to present yourself in the proper light. If you want to be successful, give careful attention to everything about you and everything you do. Make sure that your customers see you in the way you want them to see you.

If you present yourself as warm and approachable, as competent and capable, as sincere and trustworthy, and genuinely interested in your customer, you can open the door to do business.

Learn to Speak, Not Just to Talk

Notice that I named speaking, not talking, as one of the three skills of effective communication. Parrots can talk. To speak is to talk with a purpose.

To speak is to organize your words in a manner calculated to achieve a purpose, and to season those words with voice qualities, facial expressions, and body language that reinforce them with power and persuasion.

Good communicators don't try to impress people with their vocabularies; neither do they try to fake regional or ethnic accents just to try to cozy up to people. If a regional or ethnic vernacular comes natural to you, and you're talking to someone who would respond favorably to it, go ahead and use it. But remember that standard English is always safe and always appropriate. People who try to fake accents usually sound like fakes. And if you sound like a fake, people will assume you're a fake.

The best words are the familiar words that you and your prospects use in your daily lives. Choose short, strong words to convey your presentation. Organize your thoughts ahead of time. If you have your thoughts clearly in mind, your words will flow naturally. Rehearsing your presentations allows you to become familiar with them. Rehearse them mentally as well as orally. Imagine the things you'll say. Imagine your prospect's objections. And imagine how you will overcome those objections. If your mind can see yourself making your presentation smoothly, effectively, and successfully, you're more likely to be smooth, effective, and successful in reality.

Loud and Fast Doesn't Get the Sales

We're all familiar with the stereotype of the fast-talking salesperson. We also know that it's a negative stereotype. People who talk at a machine-gun pace make their listeners nervous. People also put more confidence in a low-pitched voice. A low-pitched voice tells the prospect that you're in control of your thoughts and feelings. A high-pitched voice conveys a sense that you're losing control of a situation. Deliver your presentations at a comfortable pace, in a calm but enthusiastic voice, using the lower end of your voice range. Speak loud enough to convey confidence and to allow your prospect to hear you comfortably. But don't shout.

Some salespeople appear to think that the louder and faster they talk, the more likely they are to make the sale. Such salespeople have problems paying their bills. Professional salespeople learn the difference between talking and speaking. They know that they're not there to coerce; they're there to achieve mind-to-mind orientation.

You're Not Making Social Calls

Professional salespeople also know that they are not in the business of making social calls. They don't drop by a customer's home or place of business just to chat.

Of course, they are always pleasant and friendly. But people expect to be sold. They expect a salesperson to sell them on the value of a product or service, and to assure them of the reliability of the company. If you're not there to do that, you're just taking up your prospect's valuable time.

I once talked with an old pro who represented one of the largest furniture manufacturers in the United States. He was so well-liked by the people in his territory that when his company named him "Salesman of the Year," his customers got together and gave him an appreciation dinner.

When I asked him the secret of his success, he said, "I have never been in a furniture store without my briefcase. When I walk in the door, they know I'm there to do business."

The professional salesperson opens the door to speak about business and then keeps the interview on track.

If you want to build your sales/communication skills, learn to speak effectively, learn to organize what you will say, and then stick to your presentation.

Listen Your Way to Success

Part two of the SLO principle of effective communication is listening.

Notice that I didn't say "hearing."

You *hear* the noise of traffic. You *hear* the background music in an elevator. You *hear* the jet as it goes over your head.

But you *listen* for the sound of a ping in your engine. You *listen* to the cry of a baby to determine whether it's a cry of distress or a cry for attention. You *listen* when you ask someone for directions. And you *listen* when your prospects tell you what's on their minds.

Listening is to hearing what speaking is to talking. Hearing is the natural response of your ears to sound. But listening is using your ears and your mind to absorb and understand what your prospect is saying. If you're a professional salesperson and an effective communicator, you listen to your prospect.

If you listen—really listen—you invest yourself in the concerns and needs of your prospect. In an increasingly high-tech world, people are becoming alienated, and they respond positively to salespeople who show them that they care. And one great way to do that is to listen.

Active listening is important in effective communication for a number of reasons:

♦ *It shows that you are genuinely interested in your prospect.*

You can't pay close attention to someone you're not interested in. When prospects perceive that you're sincerely interested in what *they* have to say, they'll respond with interest to what *you* have to say. Listen to the prospect if you want the prospect to listen to you.

♦ *When you listen, you learn.*

You learn valuable information that can help you close the sale. You learn what the prospect needs and what the prospect wants; you can even learn what the prospect *doesn't* want.

Through listening, you learn what excites your prospect the most. In sales terms, you find your client's hot button.

♦ *You discover false impressions the prospect may have about you, your company, or your product, and you can correct them.*

A submarine finds its way through the dark ocean deep by sending out sound waves—sonar. These waves bounce off objects and rebound toward the submarine. But sending the signal is only half the job. If nobody is there to hear the echoes, the submarine is navigating blindly. If the sonar operator doesn't know what to listen for, the navigator may mistake a whale for another submarine—or worse yet, another submarine for a whale.

A salesperson who doesn't learn to listen is similarly navigating blindly. Conversation is a two-way process. You speak and your prospect responds. By listening skillfully to the response, you can judge whether the prospect understood your message accurately. You can pick up on obstacles in the way of the sale. You can distinguish real obstacles from apparent obstacles, and adjust your message accordingly.

Learn the Three Basics of Listening

Listening involves three basic elements: interpretation, evaluation, and reaction.

Interpretation entails looking for the meaning of what the prospect is telling you. As you listen, you put yourself in the prospect's shoes and try to interpret what you hear from the prospect's point of view. You look for thoughts and feelings.

Then, you fit what you hear into the framework of what you already know, and evaluate it against your present knowledge. Ask questions for clarification, and listen carefully to the answers. Then, give your reaction.

Some salespeople let their minds rush ahead of the prospect's words. When they think they know what the prospect is going to say, they tune out the rest of the message. They're more interested in rebutting prospects than they are in understanding them. Savvy salespeople don't prejudge. They try to anticipate the direction of the prospect's thinking, but they try to absorb everthing that's being said. Their purpose is to understand prospects, not to prove them wrong. They follow the prospect through the thinking process.

If you do this, you'll learn what the prospect needs and wants, and you'll be in better position to find an answer to those needs and wants.

A good listener isn't necessarily a silent listener. Asking questions is an important part of the active listening process. But you're not out to grill or cross-examine the prospect. Your questions should be used to help the prospect provide the information you want. Keep them brief and open-ended.

Good Listeners Give Feedback

Good listeners also provide their prospects with feedback. They let them know they're listening by nodding occasionally or responding with "unh huh" or "I see." They also occasionally paraphrase what their prospects have told them. This gives prospects a chance to correct any misinterpretation.

◆ *You involve your prospect in the selling process.*

No matter what you're selling, you'll lose the sale if you focus primarily on the product. The center of your attention has to be the prospect and the prospect has to be involved in the selling process. You're not looking for ways to sell a product; you're looking for ways to help your customer.

Look at the commercials on television and note how they involve the customer. Soft-drink commercials don't focus on the superior flavor of the drink. They focus on people having fun, and they show their products contributing to the overall enjoyment.

Kodak created a desire for its product by encouraging people to "trust your memories to Kodak." Hewlett-Packard didn't try to sell its computers; it sold "solutions to unusual problems."

Think of your prospects first; then think of ways you can make your products and services useful or enjoyable to them. Use friendly questions to learn what the customer's desires and wants are. Then, look for ways to fulfill them.

If you can get your prospect physically involved with your product, that's great. A test drive in a new car can do more than the most eloquent words to make a prospect fall in love with the product. Look for ways to give your prospect the equivalent of that test drive.

Learn to Observe

Part three of the SLO formula is to observe.

Notice that the word is *observe,* not *see.*

Seeing is the natural response of your eyes to visual images. Observing is paying attention to the signals your prospect is sending. Observing is to seeing what listening is to hearing and speaking is to talking.

Effective sales communicators learn to look for buying signals—those subtle messages that indicate that it's time to start the close. They observe the signs of confusion that say, "Tell me more." They watch the facial expressions that indicate distraction or lack of interest. Real pros can sense the slightest changes of mood and interpret those as an indication to move into a new phase of the presentation.

When a signal says something is going right, the professional salesperson can build on it to move toward the target—closing the sale, getting the order.

Listening With the Eyes

Here are some common visual signals to "listen for" with the eyes:

◆ *The prospect won't look you in the eye.* People who have low opinions of themselves often find it hard to look people in the eye, so when the prospect avoids eye contact it could be because of low self-esteem. But it can also indicate that the prospect is not being truthful. Remember how hard it was to look your mother in the eye and say, "It wasn't me that ate all the cookies"? Few people are brazen enough to look you in the eye while lying. But be careful about concluding that your prospect is being untruthful, especially if the prospect comes from a different culture. In some cultures, direct eye contact is considered rude.

◆ *The prospect tries to force eye contact.* Sincere people don't usually try to force you to look them in the eye. Forced eye contact may mean that your prospect is faking it.

◆ *The prospect rubs one eye.* This could mean that the prospect is having trouble inwardly accepting what you're saying. When your prospect says "Sounds good to me," while rubbing one eye, you may want to ask a few questions to find out what the reservations are and how you can remove them from the prospect's mind.

◆ *The prospect's feet are tapping.* When prospects tap their feet while talking, it usually means that they're not too sure of what they're saying. If you notice feet tapping while the prospect says "We'll have the financing in place by the time you're ready to deliver," don't bet your monthly commission that the money will be there when the goods arrive.

◆ *The prospect looks at you with a long, crooked smile.* When people smile, the mouth usually curves into a pleasant arc that curves equally on both sides of the face. Most facial expressions change from moment to moment. If your prospect's smile is a bit crooked and remains fixed for more than a moment or two, it's probably not a genuine smile. Be wary of what you're being told.

◆ *The prospect's fingers are rubbing together.* When you see the prospect's thumb and forefinger rubbing together, it often means that some information is being withheld. It may be a signal for you to ask some penetrating questions.

◆ *The prospect stares and blinks.* If you've made your best presentation and the prospect stares at the ceiling and blinks rapidly, the deal is under consideration. Allow your prospect time to decide. If you hear a deep breath and a sigh, the decision has probably been made.

These examples are just guidelines and shouldn't be taken as absolute indications of what the prospect is thinking. Prospects may rub their eyes because they didn't get enough sleep and are trying to come awake; or they may have a speck of dust in them. If toes are tapping, listen to make sure they're not responding to the catchy beat of a song on the radio. The important thing is to remain observant. If you pay careful attention, you'll pick up on the signs of sincerity and insincerity instinctively, and they'll become a part of your selling savvy.

Five SLO Tips

Here are five tips to enable you to follow the SLO method of communicating and to increase your sales:

(1) *Be specific in your own communication.*

What we're talking about is targeted communication.

Some people use the shotgun approach to communicating. They walk into prospects' offices talking about everything from weather to politics. They talk as fast as they can for as long as the prospects will listen.

When they finish, they leave everybody, including their prospects, confused about who they are and what they are selling. All their prospects know for sure is that these salespersons are big talkers. Maybe even interesting, entertaining talkers.

Professional salespeople use a targeted communication approach. They know they will have only one good shot per prospect, so they organize what they will say.

They plan what they will present and practice the way they will say it. Once they're with their prospects, they zero in on their targets. And their target in each case is to close the sale.

Those who become successful salespeople learn to target everything they say and do toward one goal—getting the order.

(2) *Keep returning to the main purpose: the sale.*

When you're talking with someone—anyone, not just a prospect—it's very easy to get lost rambling.

You notice a picture of the prospect's family on the wall, and you comment. The next thing you know, the prospect is telling you everything about little Charlotte, the star of her Little League team.

When that happens, you have to bring the prospect tactfully back to the subject at hand—your product and how that product can help the prospect.

Ever so gently, the effective communicator constantly brings the topic of conversation back to the main theme of the presentation.

(3) *Be interesting.*

It won't do anyone any good if you put your prospects to sleep.

Look alive. Use words that are charged with energy. Use strong selling words, such as *value, solution, proven,* and *reliable.* Be clear when talking to prospects, and use examples and illustrations that your prospects can understand—examples and illustrations that relate to their frame of reference and level of awareness.

If you're selling to a business person, use business-related examples. If you're making a presentation to a homemaker, use household examples.

Get excited, get enthusiastic, and get motivated to move your prospects to productive action.

(4) *Be alert to buying signals.*

Buying signals can be anything the prospect does or says that indicates an interest in owning what you sell. These include facial expressions, gestures, body movements, words, and questions. The strength of your close depends on your ability to recognize these signals and then to act on them.

A signal could be a simple statement: "My old copier is in bad shape."

Or it could be a question: "Do you charge for installation?" "Will you train the operator?" "Do you have a finance plan?" "Does it come in red?" "How much space would it take on my counter?"

Questions such as those are often the best indicators of buying interest. But body language can also convey important signals. Look for facial expressions to change from doubt to agreement or from a frown to a smile.

When a prospect's arms drop from a folded position, or the prospect leans forward and shows an interest in the features or proofs you present, it's safe to consider these to be positive buying signals.

You can also trigger a signal by asking a question that causes the prospect to comment or react.

Verbal and non-verbal signals appear at all stages of your presentation. Watch for them.

(5) *Focus on your prospect.*

This tip ties together all the other communication pointers. The professional salesperson tunes into prospects and customers, talks about what each one is interested in, listens to the concerns expressed, and watches all reactions and movements.

The professional realizes that the key to communicating successfully with prospects is to get completely involved with them and their needs and concerns.

FIVE DEADLY SINS OF SELLING

The savvy salesperson must also be aware of a few don'ts. Let's look at some mistakes that are deadly for sales.

(1) *Ignoring people during your presentation.*

This is the number-one communication mistake most salespeople make.

A professional realizes that everyone involved in a presentation can make or break the sale. If you direct your attention only to the most important person present, you may offend someone who has a great deal of influence over this person. Treat everyone equally and with equal interest.

(2) *Doing all the talking.*

Customer feedback is a vital part of selling. Not only does monopolizing the conversation bore your prospect; it may also cause you to miss important signals or information from the prospect—things that could help you close the sale.

(3) *Rambling or continually repeating yourself.*

Don't take forever to make your point. Once you've made it, be quiet and let your prospect respond. The longer you talk after making your point, the more likely you are to talk your prospect right out of a sale.

(4) *Boasting about your own personal achievements.*

Don't brag about what a great salesperson you are. Let your prospects judge for themselves.

Don't brag about your personal exploits either. The prospect is unlikely to be interested in that big shark you caught last weekend and doesn't want to hear how you broke 80 on the golf course or birdied that difficult hole.

It can be very useful to talk about satisfied clients, but be careful not to brag. Saying, "I've never had a customer who didn't want one of these gadgets," is like challenging the prospect to say "You've just encountered your first one."

(5) *Saying something the prospect may find offensive.*

Using off-color language or ethnic jokes can have the same effect on people as pouring cold water in their laps. It might get their attention, but it's not likely to make them hear more of what you have to say.

When you are talking with your prospects remember this: Effective communication is a two-way exchange of information that produces a desired response.

That's also a great definition of selling.

You exchange information with a client in a way that motivates the client to buy.

The single most important way to boost your selling power and your income is to become more effective in communication. You can do that by sharpening your speaking, listening, and observing skills, all of which are vital parts of selling savvy.

Remember: The better you become at communicating, the better you can become at selling.

Check Your Selling Savvy

I. List five characteristics of effective sales communication:

    (1) _____

    (2) _____

    (3) _____

    (4) _____

    (5) _____

II. List the three elements in the SLO communication formula:

    (1) _____

    (2) _____

    (3) _____

III. Check one: ( )Non-verbal communication ( ) Verbal communication makes up 93% of the total messages we communicate.

IV. What is the difference between talking and speaking?

    _____

V. What is the difference between seeing and observing?

    _____

VI. List four benefits from active listening:

    (1) _____

    (2) _____

(3) _____

(4) _____

VII. List five useful tips for following the SLO formula:

(1) _____

(2) _____

(3) _____

(4) _____

(5) _____

6

Working Smart Beats Working Hard

Salespeople often say to me, "Nido, I'm working as hard as I can, but I don't seem to be getting anywhere."

Have you ever started your day with a pile of paper in front of you awaiting your action, then worked your head off during the day with nothing to show for your efforts but a bigger pile of paper?

Have you ever started out knowing that you had a whole list of important calls to make, only to find at the end of the day that you had worked hard at everything but making those calls?

If you have, maybe it's time you quit working so hard and started working smarter.

The professional with selling savvy knows that the key to success is not how hard you work but how smart you work.

Your Most Valuable Asset

Working smart means making the highest and best use of your most precious asset.

Sometimes, I ask people at sales seminars to name their most important asset. Many say it's their talent—their ability to sell.

Talent can be developed, and ability can be acquired. But the most important asset you have comes in a limited quantity that can't be increased and can't be stretched. If you're going to be a successful salesperson, you must learn to use it wisely and effectively.

We're talking about time.

It doesn't matter how good you are at selling if you let your best opportunities slip away from you because you don't have enough time to cash in on them.

THREE WAYS TO SPEND TIME

How wisely do you invest your time?

If you often find yourself saying, "I could make more calls if I just had more time," you may be squandering your most precious and limited resource.

The bad news is that you can't make more time: Each hour has only 60 minutes, each day only 24 hours, and each week only seven days. The good news is that you don't need to.

You can spend your precious time on three types of effort:

(1) *Things that lie beyond your range of effective action.*

It's great to be ambitious, but it's a waste of time to attempt the impossible. Don't try selling snow cones to Eskimos or fur coats to Fiji Islanders.

(2) *Things that you can accomplish easily enough, but that don't lead you toward your objectives.*

This is called wheel spinning. It happens when you use all your clever strategies to get an appointment with the CEO, only to learn that the CEO delegates all buying decisions to the director of purchasing. It happens when you devote precious time to selling to a business that's being phased out and offers no chance for future sales and no opportunity for cross selling.

(3) *Things that you can accomplish and that take you toward your objectives.*

These are the activities you want to devote the major portion of your time to. These are the important activities.

Some people spend far more time on urgent tasks than they do on important tasks. There's a big difference. Urgent tasks are things you have to do immediately to avoid some kind of crisis. Important tasks are the things that move you toward your goals.

Nip Problems in the Bud

You can minimize the attention you need to pay to urgent tasks by taking care of problems before they become urgent. Little problems become big problems when you fail to take care of them at the outset. That big, frisky kitten out there scaring the chickens may be annoying but harmless. But give it a couple of years to grow and it becomes a lion carrying off sheep. Minor customer complaints may be nothing but nuisances, but let them accumulate without attending to them and soon a major customer has defected to a competitor.

You can take two simple steps that will enable you to use your time more effectively attending to important things. If you'll try them, you'll find that you have more time than you ever imagined.

FIRST STEP: MAKE A SCHEDULE

The first step is to put yourself on a schedule.

Many salespeople hate schedules.

"Schedules tie me down," they say. "They're too restrictive."

Occasionally, somebody says, "I need space to be creative."

But schedules can be liberating. What happens if you don't put yourself on a schedule? You constantly find yourself caught up in responding to what others want you to do. You react to all the little emergencies that seem to crop up everywhere. These little emergencies and these requests from others can end up dictating your schedule. You're following one, but it isn't your own.

If you're really serious about increasing your sales, one of the most productive things you can do is to put yourself on a schedule and stick to it. When you do that, you take charge of your career.

First, decide what you want to accomplish. Choose your own objectives. Then, create a schedule that will allow you to meet those objectives in the least amount of time.

A fixed schedule will greatly simplify your life. It will bring about two major benefits.

First, it will force you to fit your daily routine into a time pattern. That time pattern will help you to put your waking hours to their most productive use.

Second, it will encourage you to keep a written reminder of everything you need to accomplish. This can be very helpful, since the more successful you become, the more tasks and ideas you'll have to remember.

Some Pointers to Help You With Scheduling

Developing a schedule and sticking to it is not that difficult. Here are some pointers:

(1) *Keep a daily "to do" list.*

At the end of every day, write a list of all the things you need to accomplish the next day. Organize your "to do" list by the priority of each item.

It's impossible to remember everything you need to do and still focus your full attention on your prospects, unless you learn to live by a "to do" list.

Charles Schwab, the great steel tycoon of a bygone era, adopted this approach and made a $10 million sale the first day he used it. From then on, he was a devout believer in "to do" lists. They really work.

(2) *Never allow yourself to be detoured from a scheduled activity.*

If you are in the middle of a task on your "to do" list, don't let meaningless interruptions distract you.

Real emergencies will arise and disrupt your schedule. But don't lose valuable minutes because of worthless distractions. When I say "worthless" distractions, I mean interruptions that are not going to earn you income.

How many times have you been trapped into a 20-minute discussion because someone innocently asked you, "Do you have a minute?"

No one ever wants "a minute" of your time. People will take as much time as you give them.

Professional salespeople break their hours down into two categories: the hours that earn income, and the hours that cost them income.

Talking to an old friend on the phone for an hour costs you income. Making presentations to qualified prospects earns you income. It's as simple as that. When you give away time to distractions, you're giving away income.

(3) *Build flexibility into your schedule.*

Delayed or canceled appointments go with the job of selling. But you can turn waiting time into productive time.

If you know the delay will last more than 15 minutes, don't wait around. Leave a polite note saying you will schedule another appointment. Then, check your "to do" list and move on to the next item.

If you must wait, look on your "to do" list for something you can take care of while you wait. If you don't find anything else you can do, go back over your presentation, read product-information reports, or do some important paperwork. What you can't afford to do is to waste your time reading three-year-old magazines in the waiting area.

(4) *Use deadlines to eliminate procrastination.*

I've known salespeople who put burglar alarms on everything—their cars, their luggage, hotel doors, and their homes. They were afraid someone was going to steal something valuable from them. Yet, they paid no attention to the most clever thief of all—procrastination. And we have all been its victims at one time or another.

We say, "I need to call on that prospect one of these days," "I've got to settle that customer's complaint soon," or "I've got to update my samples and catalogs when I get around to it."

But "one of these days," "soon," and "when I get around to it" all have a two-word synonym: too late.

Somehow, we kid ourselves into believing that we will have more time later. Or we convince ourselves that, if we put it off, an unpleasant task will become more pleasant.

Yet, there never seems to be more time. And usually, the unpleasant task becomes even more unpleasant the longer we put it off.

When you're selling, procrastination can cost you dearly. For example, if you put off getting a prospect's signature on an order, your competitor can come by and close the sale that should have been yours.

You can conquer procrastination. Put teeth into your schedule by setting deadlines for everything you do. When something you need to do comes to mind, do it immediately, if you can. If you can't, write a deadline into your schedule for that task.

Someone once said, "You don't judge people by what they start; you judge them by what they finish."

(5) *Guard against bad habits that waste time.*

Keep a constant vigil against habits such as:

- Leaving your home, office, or hotel late.
- Making regular social calls on good accounts.
- Making too many return calls on poor prospects.

- Ignoring the fact that many of your prospects are in their offices before eight, after five, and on weekends.
- Spending three hours of potential action time to take an old friend to lunch.

All these habits waste time. We need to avoid them and constantly guard against them.

(6) *Guard your action time.*

Your action time is the time you actually spend in the presence of qualified buyers.

Keep in mind two important principles about action time.

First, make your action time count. Don't waste one second of one minute. Move the client toward your goals as quickly as possible. But be careful not to make the client feel rushed or pressured.

Second, always work toward increasing your action time. You can do that in several ways:

- Build more and more action time into your schedule.
- Plan carefully for all sales calls so you can make every minute count.
- Handle service calls by telephone, and do as much selling by phone as you can.
- Use waiting time as productively as possible.

Professional salespeople realize that the best time to reach most prospects is between 8 a.m. and 5 p.m., Monday through Friday. That's why they reserve almost all that time for presentations and interviews with customers and prospects.

Goal-setting, strategizing, and paperwork are important, but all those things can be done after five, or on weekends.

So don't burn up your most valuable time with such tasks as filing orders or having your car serviced. You can handle those jobs any time.

STEP TWO: GET ORGANIZED

The second step in managing your time more effectively is to get organized. You can organize many areas of your life.

(1) *Organize your paperwork.*

How much time do you spend searching for important materials or notes because your paperwork is not organized?

Organize your desk, your car, your office, and even your luggage, so you know precisely where everything is. Keep samples and catalogs neatly stored for easy access.

Don't be a paper shuffler; be a paper processor. Don't let your desk become a miniature landfill. It should be a work area, not a storage area for papers you don't quite know what to do with.

When I go through my morning mail, I usually arrange it into three stacks. One is for papers that call for personal action by me. One is for papers that need to be referred to others for action. The other is for paper that needs to be filed. The paper that needs to be filed goes to a secretary, who knows where to put it. The paper that needs to be referred to others goes to the other parties, with appropriate notes. Then, I take the paper that requires my personal action, one piece at a time, and I act.

When I'm through, my desk is clear and I'm ready to make the highest and best use of my time.

(2) *Organize your travel time.*

Always map out your travel plans on paper—before you leave. Look for the shortest routes. And schedule appointments close together. That way, you won't waste a lot of time crisscrossing the city or territory.

When you're on a plane, a train, or a bus, use your travel time for reading or doing paperwork.

If you get tied up in traffic, don't waste your time swearing at the driver in front of you. Listen to a cassette or critique your last presentation. Use the time to think through an idea. Or use your car phone for prospecting or setting up more appointments.

(3) *Organize your presentations.*

Professionals know what points they want to cover, and for maximum impact, they cover them in the least possible time.

It is a waste of your time—and your prospect's time—if you have to fumble for ideas, words, or materials while you're making a presentation.

It helps to know your customer's buying potential so you can budget more time with likely big spenders, and less time with little spenders.

If you think of your time in terms of money, it makes sense to spend more time with the people who are able to spend more money.

Make it your business to know your customer's needs before you begin your presentation. That way you can focus on the issues that interest the prospect most and not waste time on low-priority concerns.

(4) *Organize your appointments in order of priority.*

There are several methods of grading your prospects. A good one is to imagine yourself as the home team moving a ball across a football field. You're on your own goal line when you make a cold call. Each subsequent call should move you closer to the end zone at the other end of the field. Through presentations, meetings, and conversations, you move the prospect across the 100 yards that leads to pay dirt. When you're on the prospect's goal line, the sale is imminent.

If you're a good salesperson, you'll have prospects all over the field. Some may be on your own 20-yard line. Some may be at the 50-yard line. Some may be on the prospect's 10.

The closer you are to the prospect's goal line, the better the appointment is. You stand a much better chance of closing that sale.

So don't spend most of your time chasing people who are on your own 10 or 20 when you have some prospects with the ball close to their end zones. Spend the biggest chunk of your time pursuing the people who are closest to buying.

Of course, some time has to be spent cultivating new business. But don't spend so much time pursuing less-certain prospects that you lose sight of those who are ready to buy.

HOW TO BOOST THE VALUE OF YOUR APPOINTMENTS

Here are several other things you can do to boost the value of your appointments:

- ◆ Set up appointments at times and places that are convenient for you, as well as for your prospects.
- ◆ Be sure a decision maker is present. Otherwise, you may be wasting your time.
- ◆ Avoid tying your appointment to a meal, where you don't have the option of leaving as soon as you have finished with your business.

Don't Let the Clock Bully You

For professional salespeople, time management is a way of life. They don't let their clocks bully them.

Time wasters, on the other hand, become slaves to the clock. They rush around like crazy, trying to get everything done. They let their time manage them.

If you use a little selling savvy, you'll be able to get much more done in less time.

Just put yourself on a schedule and organize your work, and you will find you have all the time you need.

Develop a Sense of Urgency

Let me wind up this chapter with one of the most savvy time-management secrets I've ever discovered.

It's simply this: Develop a sense of urgency about everything you do.

When you have a sense of urgency, every action becomes a step toward the completion of a sale. With a sense of urgency, you always operate with a consciousness of closure.

A consciousness of closure is a constant drive to finish whatever you start. It's a constant search for ways to shorten the sales cycle.

The sales cycle is the length of time it takes to move from discovering a prospect to wrapping up the sale. Sometimes, it seems as though that process meets with one delay after another; that we are always one step away from closing the sale.

For instance, we've all had prospects say to us, "Send me some material on this, and I'll get back to you." What they really mean is, "Don't bother me; I'm not interested enough to act on that right now."

Cut to the Action

With a sense of urgency, we're always thinking in terms of bringing everything to a concrete action. We move in quickly and find out whether the prospect who says "I'll get back to you" really needs more information to make a decision, or is simply throwing up a smoke screen.

If the prospect wants more information, we need to find out specifically what information is needed and supply it right away.

But if the statement, "I'll get back to you," is just a smoke screen, we have to find out the real reason the prospect is not ready to act.

Here's another one of those typical delays: A prospect says, "Send me a contract and I'll look it over." That means absolutely nothing.

The professional salesperson will say, "If I send this to you tomorrow, are you going to be there to receive it?"

The prospect may answer, "Well, no, I won't be back in the office until Thursday."

Then, the salesperson needs to say, "OK, I'll send it through overnight mail so it will arrive in your office Thursday. And will you be able to okay it Thursday and put it in the return mail that day?"

Nail Down That Commitment

A sense of urgency pushes you to get a commitment that says, "Yes, we are going to do this at a specific time."

Almost all buying decisions are made within 24 hours of the time they are proposed. The longer you let a prospect mull over a purchase, the lower your chances are of making a sale, and the more of your time it eats up.

Professional salespeople understand the importance of looking for ways to shorten the sales cycle. They are constantly trying to tie up all the loose ends of every part of each transaction.

Your Time Is Your Money

So be aware of the value of your time.

Never say, "I was in the area, so I thought I'd just drop in."

That's telling your customer that your time is not really important. It's also saying, "Your business is not very important either. I came by only because I happened to be in the neighborhood; I wouldn't have made a special trip to call on you."

Smart salespeople also avoid saying, "My time is your time." When you say that, you're not being professional. You're enslaving yourself to the customer's schedule and priorities.

For salespeople more than for anyone else, time is money. So when you say, "My time is your time," you're actually saying, "My money is your money."

The key to sales success is to invest every minute of every day of every week as wisely as possible.

It's a big part of selling savvy.

CHECK YOUR SELLING SAVVY

I. What are the three basic categories of effort on which you can spend your time?

    (1) _____

    (2) _____

    (3) _____

II. What is the difference between an ***urgent*** task and an ***important*** task?

    _____

    _____

III. How can you prevent urgent tasks from crowding out important tasks?

    _____

    _____

IV. What two steps can help you make time for important things?

    (1) _____

    (2) _____

V. List six pointers for setting a schedule and sticking to it:

    (1) _____

    (2) _____

    (3) _____

    (4) _____

(5) _____

(6) _____

VI. Name four basic areas in which you can organize your efforts:

(1) _____

(2) _____

(3) _____

(4) _____

VII. Name three ways to boost the value of your appointments:

(1) _____

(2) _____

(3) _____

CHAPTER 7

Become a Consultant to Your Customers

Dale Carnegie once called Frank Bettger the best salesperson he'd ever met. Carnegie said Bettger could sell almost anything to almost anybody.

And what was Bettger's secret of success in selling?

Let Bettger himself tell you:

"The one biggest secret of selling anything is: Try to find out what people want, and then help them get it."

That's a powerful insight. It's also a valuable specimen of selling savvy.

How to Help People Get What They Want

In this chapter, we'll explore ways to apply that bit of savvy toward making you a very successful salesperson, while you help people get what they want.

Most salespeople approach selling from the opposite position: They decide what they want to sell, then they try to talk people into buying it. That's almost guaranteed to create sales resistance. It puts the ball in the prospect's court. It tells prospects, in effect, "Here's why I think you ought to buy this product. Now tell me why you shouldn't."

And since you're asking your prospects to transfer money from their hands to yours, they're usually pretty good at thinking of reasons for not doing it. But if your prospects perceive that you're holding something they want, they'll look for reasons to move what they want out of your hands and into theirs.

You're Not Selling Products and Services

The problem is that most salespeople believe that their customers want to buy the products and services they are selling. They think customers want to buy automobiles, insurance, clothing, or some other item.

You acquire selling savvy when you acquire this insight: Your prospects don't want the products or services you're selling. They want the things those products or services can do for them.

Many salespeople argue over whether it's easier to sell tangibles or intangibles. But the salesperson with sales savvy and business acumen knows that we are all selling intangibles.

People Don't Just Buy Suits

Think about the way you approach buying a new suit. Certainly, you are looking for clothing, but if that's all you're buying you can get by with a loincloth or a burlap bag with armholes.

But you're looking for more than basic covering. Your real buying decision will be made on factors such as how a suit makes you look, how it makes you feel about yourself, and how it fits your lifestyle and personality.

Those are all very intangible factors. They have to do with your perceptions, your needs, your feelings, and your values. The fact is that you're not simply buying a suit of clothes; you're buying what that suit will do for you.

And here's where selling savvy really comes into play. You might know exactly what you want your new suit to do for you. But if the person trying to sell you a suit doesn't understand what you want and doesn't show you what you want, you won't buy—no matter what the salesperson says or does.

On the other hand, you might not know clearly what you want a suit to do for you, or what kind of suit will produce the results you desire. The salesperson's challenge then becomes to help you understand what you want and how to get it.

An amateur might try to sell you by lowering the price, by trying to convince you that your expectations are wrong, or even by trying to manipulate you into buying a suit you don't like.

But the professional—the salesperson with savvy—knows that all those tactics are a waste of time.

Think of Yourself as a Consultant

If you want to be successful in sales, you have to think of yourself as a consultant for your customer. Consultants are people who carefully study their prospects' needs, concerns, and desires, then show them how to get what they want.

Consultants focus first on solving the client's most pressing problem or fulfilling the client's greatest desire. But to become a true consultant, you have to go beyond making the first sale.

Real professionals understand a very important principle of selling savvy: Satisfied clients make the best prospects for future sales.

Therefore, selling professionals target all their efforts at establishing long-term relationships with their customers. They think of them as clients. They see themselves not only as providers of quality goods and services, but also as invaluable resources of information and expert counsel.

Professionals perceive themselves as experts who can offer valuable insights and solutions to their customers' problems. And they work hard to instill in their prospects that same perception.

Developing this kind of solid relationship with a customer offers substantial rewards.

A $50 MILLION RELATIONSHIP

One of the most dramatic illustrations of how this works is a decision Lee Iacocca made when he moved to the Chrysler Corporation.

When he took control of the company, one of his first moves was to dismiss the two advertising agencies that were handling the Chrysler account.

He replaced them with the agency he had worked with so successfully at Ford.

As Iacocca put it, he didn't have enough time to acclimate Chrysler's agencies to his way of thinking. It was much simpler for him to bring along an agency he had worked with before. It was a $50 million decision that resulted in the largest single transfer of an advertising account ever recorded.

That agency had become much more to Iacocca than just another advertising company. To Iacocca, that agency was an indispensable ally—a valuable consulting resource.

The salesperson with selling savvy understands the value of such a relationship with a customer and strives to maintain that relationship.

The Secret Lies in Positioning

But how do you establish such a relationship? How do you turn prospects and customers into loyal clients?

Think back to our discussion of positioning in Chapter Two. Positioning is the key to establishing a solid relationship with customers.

Professional salespeople position themselves as expert advisers to their prospects. They prove by their actions that they are trying not just to sell to their prospects but also to help them get what they want.

Positioning yourself as your customers' consultant enables you to establish and maintain secure, long-term relationships with them. It's the best way to build the kind of solid client base and repeat business that can provide security and steady growth—for you and your company.

Become a Consultant to Your Customers

Let's explore two of the central elements of building permanent—and profitable—consulting relationships with your clients.

THE FIRST ELEMENT: BECOME AN EXPERT

If you want to earn the respect and confidence of your prospects, you have to position yourself as an expert. An expert is defined as "a person who is very skillful or highly trained and informed in some special field."

Translated to the sales field, experts are competent professionals who are knowledgeable about selling, about their companies and their products, about their industries, about their competition, and about each of their clients.

How do you achieve this level of professionalism? Here are six pointers:

(1) *Become an expert in your field.*

Professionals don't just act as if they're experts; they *are* experts. They make it their business to know everything there is to know about their business.

If you want your customers to see you as an expert, you must be an expert salesperson.

To become a consulting salesperson, you have to become so familiar with the selling process that you can concentrate totally on planning, strategizing, and developing other areas of expertise.

Think about your knowledge of the selling basics next time you watch Olympic ice skaters perform on television. They perform the most difficult of movements with such style and grace that they make it look easy.

Their movements are elegance in motion. When they make a mistake or their routine is interrupted, they pick right up and keep going.

That kind of excellence comes only from practice. They have drilled and drilled until they have mastered the fundamentals so thoroughly that they don't even have to think about them.

So when the spotlight is on them, they are free to concentrate on expression, on timing, and on communicating with their audiences.

The sales professional has the same kind of command over the basics of selling. The essentials are so ingrained that the professional performs without thinking about them.

(2) *Become an expert on your company.*

If you want to become your customer's consultant, you must become an expert on your company.

As a salesperson, you may be the only representative of your company that your customers ever see. When customers see you, they're looking at your company, as far as they're concerned. If they like you, they'll like the company. If they distrust you, they'll distrust the company.

Trust is a vital part of any relationship. Competent professionals know how to build their customers' confidence in their companies.

Major corporations spend millions of dollars advertising their brand names. They realize that people buy from companies they know and trust.

The more you know about your company, the more you're able to give information that will inspire confidence in new prospects and keep your regular customers loyal.

(3) *Become an expert on what you sell.*

Knowing as much as possible about the products and services you sell is the third vital area in which the consulting salesperson must have some expertise.

When customers ask, "How many units can it produce per minute?," "How much floor space will it take up?," or "How soon can you ship it?," they want information, not sales puff.

One of the most common complaints consumers and professional buyers make is that they can't get straight answers to the simple questions they ask salespeople.

The main reason they don't get straight answers is that the salespeople don't know enough about their products or services to provide the answers.

We owe it to our customers to have the information to provide quick and concise answers to at least 99% of the questions they might ask.

In fact, what you know about your complete product line and all of the services your company offers is one of the best measures of your professionalism as a salesperson.

Professionals are inquisitive. They ask questions and are always eager to learn. They know that knowledge is like money in the bank: It pays to have it, and it pays to use it.

Some salespeople like to dance around the questions with fancy footwork. If they don't know the answers, they fake them. If they're dealing with knowledgeable businesspeople, they'll find themselves on the canvas quickly. Today's customers are informed, and they don't waste time or money on people who play fast and loose with the facts. When you don't know the answer to a question, you'll earn respect by simply saying, "I don't know, but I'll find out and let you know right away." Today's customers are informed, and they appreciate integrity when they see it.

(4) *Become an expert on your industry.*

Professionals are constantly reviewing these questions:

♦ Who buys the products or services my company sells, and why do they buy them?
♦ How do these products contribute to the lives and businesses of the customers who buy them?
♦ How are these services and products used?
♦ What trends have affected the industry in recent years, and what trends are emerging that could affect customers in the future?

It's only when you know the answers to these and other vital questions that you can position yourself as a valuable resource for your clients. Savvy begins with knowledge. And knowledge begins with a dedication to learning.

(5) *Become an expert on your competition.*

If you want to position yourself as an expert consultant, know your competition. The more you know about your competitors, the greater your ability to sell against them.

So, ask yourself:

◆ Who are my competitors?
◆ What do they sell?
◆ How are their products inferior to ours?
◆ How are their products superior to ours?
◆ How do they sell?
◆ To whom do they sell?
◆ What do they tell my customers?
◆ What gaps are there in their product lines?

Some of your competitors are well-trained professionals, and many of them know more about you than you imagine.

Professional salespeople don't lie awake at night worrying about what's happening in their industries or what their competitors are doing. They just stay alert and observe everything that happens around them. They keep an eye on the competition.

They read trade journals, ask questions of their customers and people within their company, and study ads and sales literature from all the companies that serve their industry.

The more knowledge you have about your competition, the more likely your customers will be to respect you as a consultant, as a value-driven salesperson, and as a problem solver.

(6) *Become an expert on your customers.*

Most important of all, you must become an expert on your customers.

Become a Consultant to Your Customers

To understand what your customer wants and needs, you have to know your customer the way your family doctor knows you.

You take it for granted that your doctor understands the human anatomy and how the organs work. That's basic stuff.

But you're not just a generic specimen of the human race. You're *you*—a unique individual with your own physical and emotional makeup; your own pattern of aches and pains; maybe your own set of allergies.

You want your doctor to prescribe medicine that's appropriate for you and not for some generalized average citizen coming in off the street. If your doctor doesn't understand your unique symptoms and physical makeup, you may go home with some drug that will set off an allergic reaction or aggravate the condition it was intended to treat.

In the same way, sales professionals research each potential customer to discover the prospect's unique business or personal needs.

They draw out customers with questions. They observe everything their customers do and listen to everything they say.

A man named Louis Holden got the first donation Andrew Carnegie ever made to a school. In exactly four minutes, Dr. Holden collected $100,000 from a man who opened the interview by saying, "I don't believe in giving money to colleges."

How did he turn it around? As a consultant, he had done his homework on Andrew Carnegie. Once he understood Carnegie's deep desire to help young people get started in life, he was able to show his client how he could fulfill that desire by making a large donation to a college.

Knowing what motivates a prospect is probably the most powerful piece of information a salesperson can have. Professionals learn all they can about their prospects; then they use that information to influence them to buy.

To position yourself as an expert—as your customers' consultant—you have to *become* an expert. Expertise requires depth of knowledge and understanding, and that's something you can't fake. Customers can sense it when you know what you're talking about, and they recognize it quickly when you're talking over your head.

Becoming an expert requires dedication and effort. But until you've become one, you're minus the first key element in building a consulting relationship with your customer, and you're somewhere short of being the successful salesperson that you can be.

THE SECOND ELEMENT: GET INVOLVED WITH YOUR CUSTOMERS

The second element in building consulting relationships is to get involved with your customers.

Earlier, we learned the importance of listening to your prospects. By listening, you're able to learn what your prospects want, and you can proceed to sell it to them.

But to build consulting relationships, you must be willing to communicate with customers on a level that goes deeper than that.

To become a professional, you must become proficient at reading customers, sensing where they are coming from, and empathizing with their emotions.

You must be sensitive to what customers are feeling and thinking as well as to what they're telling you. Professionals see things from their customers' points of view and are able to empathize with the customers' experiences.

What I'm suggesting is that you relate to your customers much as a professional counselor relates to patients.

You listen to each customer intently and with concern. You respond to each with viable solutions and advice. And you build confidence by proving that your customers can rely on you for guidance.

When you can reach this level of communication and understanding with your client, you are creating a powerful trust bond.

You might call this process "creative communication."

Listening intently to your customers is the best way to achieve this deep level of understanding and, in the process, strengthen your position as your customer's consultant.

In my seminars and corporate consultations, I share many specific techniques and tactics to improve listening. Here are some important ones:

(1) *Make the decision to listen.*

If you're going to listen closely, you have to make a conscious choice to listen. If you don't, your mind will be led astray by distractions, you won't hear everything the prospect is saying, and you'll miss out on valuable information and insights. The only way to overcome distractions and really listen is to make a conscious choice to listen and then make yourself stick with that decision. When you go into a dialogue with a prospect, make an inward commitment to listen, then stick to your commitment.

Concentrate on what the prospect is saying. As each point is made, weigh the evidence for and against it. After several points have been made, review them in your mind. And be sure to tune into the prospect's non-verbal communication.

(2) *Be responsive.*

Respond to what your customers say. Ask questions and encourage them to continue. Show that you care. Nobody likes to be ignored.

(3) *Listen for feelings and ideas.*

This is how you gain a real understanding of your customers. To listen on this level means you try to sense how they're feeling about the subjects under discussion.

Is your customer pleased with past experiences with your product or company? Upset about something? Indifferent about a certain feature?

Take this a little deeper. Even in professional situations, people tend to let their moods show through. If your customer is preoccupied, maybe it's because of a pressing personal problem.

You may learn, for instance, that the prospect is worried about a sick child and can't give you full attention. In that case, be patient; be empathetic. Offer to call at another time. If you don't have the prospect's attention, it won't do you much good to continue with your sales interview.

Your goal as a consultant is to become not just a supplier of goods for your customers, but to be an ally, a friend, someone your customers will depend on.

The key to success in this area is to reach them on a level that goes beyond knowing what their needs are. You want to get to know them.

Reaching your customers' real emotions gives you a competitive edge in a market in which price differential is progressively losing its significance.

Be Willing to Invest the Effort

It takes selling savvy to position yourself as a consultant with your customers. But professionals realize the value of such relationships.

If you want to become a successful professional, be willing to invest the effort it takes to become a true expert. Then, act as a consultant—as someone who can offer more than just a good deal.

If you'll think and act like a consultant to your customers, you will earn their trust, their loyalty, and their business.

Earning customer loyalty and repeat business provides the major solid foundation for a successful career in selling. It's an important element in selling savvy.

CHECK YOUR SELLING SAVVY

I. What is supersalesman Frank Bettger's super selling secret?

_____

_____

II. What are the two principal elements of relationship building?

    (1) _____

    (2) _____

III. List six pointers for positioning yourself as an expert in your field:

    (1) _____

    (2) _____

    (3) _____

    (4) _____

    (5) _____

    (6) _____

IV. List three techniques for listening as part of creative communication:

    (1) _____

    (2) _____

    (3) _____

8

Questions Can Pave the Way to Sales

The single most useful tool of professional salespeople is the skillfully asked question.

In fact, the best way to tell run-of-the-mill salespeople from people with selling savvy is to listen to the kinds of questions they ask and the way they ask them. The right questions can lead to information that is essential for closing sales, and they can actively involve the prospect in the selling process.

In this chapter, we'll examine the value of asking the right questions at the right times. We'll discuss ways to develop greater savvy in using questions as a selling tool.

QUESTIONS TO ASK YOURSELF

The most vital questions that accomplished salespeople ask in the selling process are not the ones they ask prospects, as important as those questions are. Savvy salespeople know that the most critical questions are the ones they ask themselves.

Consciously or unconsciously, both amateurs and professionals ask themselves questions during the sales interview. But they ask different kinds of questions.

The amateur's questions are self-centered. The professional's questions are customer-centered. Let's review some of them.

(1) *Why should I spend time with this prospect?*

Professionals and amateurs often begin with the same question: "Why should I be investing my valuable action time with this prospect?"

The amateur's response is likely to be "Because I need to make a sale." Wrong answer. It represents the self-centered approach. It makes *your* satisfaction the principal objective of the sales encounter. But you're only half the equation. Prospects don't become customers just so you can make a sale. Unless you can provide a benefit for the prospect, there's no use calling. People buy for their reasons not for yours.

The customer-centered approach seeks a long-term, mutually beneficial relationship with the prospect you're calling on. Profitable sales arise from good relationships. Good relationships stem from mutually beneficial transactions.

(2) *Is this the best person to spend my time with?*

With a profitable relationship as a goal, you next ask yourself: "Is this prospect the best person for me to be spending my valuable action time with at this moment?"

You should ask that question up front, and you should keep asking it throughout the sales interview. If the answer ever comes up "No," end the interview as quickly as possible and find another prospect. Otherwise, you'll be wasting your most valuable asset—the precious time available to succeed at making sales. You'll also be wasting the prospect's time.

There's another kind of question that separates the savvy professional from the amateur.

(3) *What do I need to know?*

Amateurs keep asking themselves, "What do I need to *say,* right now, to move the sale along?" But the pros are always asking, "What do I need to *know,* right now, to move the sale along?"

There's a major difference between those two approaches.

The amateur's is the self-centered approach. When you focus on what you *say,* you're indicating that you haven't done your homework; that you're looking for some magical words that will make the prospect want to buy. That's putting the emphasis on what *you* want to happen instead of on what the *prospect* wants to happen. Asking what you need to *know* keeps the focus where it should be: on what's going on inside the prospect.

(4) *What do I need to get the prospect to do?*

Another question the pros ask themselves repeatedly while they're interviewing prospects is "What do I need to get the prospect to do right now?" That's a customer-centered question.

Amateurs keep asking themselves the self-centered "What do *I* need to do" question. Professionals know that it's what you get the prospect to do that makes the difference between success or failure.

Let's say the prospect has just agreed to see you, but only for a few minutes.

The amateur says, "Gosh, just five minutes to say what I normally say in half an hour." Then, comes the self-centered question: "What do I need to do?"

And the self-centered answer is, "I'd better start talking early and I'd better talk fast."

That's what most salespeople do under such circumstances. They rush through their presentations, and then they're rushed—empty handed—out the door. Rushed sales presentations almost never produce good results.

The savvy salesperson asks the customer-centered question: "What do I need to get the prospect to do?"

And the customer-centered answer?

"I need to convince this prospect of the need to commit the time required for me to make a thorough presentation."

(5) *How can I get the commitment?*

Your next question should be: "How can I get the commitment?"

An excellent way to do that would be to devote the few minutes the prospect has already committed to asking customer-centered questions. That'll help you determine whether you're talking to a qualified decision maker. That'll also help raise the prospect's interest level.

If you're successful, you can determine whether to pursue the prospect further, and you can gain the time commitment you need.

The secret lies in remaining customer-centered: Always focus on the action you need from the prospect. Never become preoccupied with the things *you* need to do.

QUESTIONS TO ASK YOUR PROSPECTS

Now that we've considered the questions you need to ask yourself, let's look at some questions you need to ask your prospects.

The professional salesperson knows that the selling cycle rotates through three basic questions:

(1) *Are you a qualified prospect?*

The answer to this question determines whether you should continue the interview.

(2) *"What will it take to get you to buy?"*

You can't close until you know the answer to that question.

(3) *"Are you going to buy now?"*

That's the $64 question—or the million-dollar question, or the $19.95 question, depending upon the price of what you're selling. It's the one that determines whether you'll get a return on the time you've invested.

Of course, you don't ask prospects those questions in that way, but they are the three crucial questions you want answered. They tell you whether prospects are able and likely to buy, what it will take to turn them into customers, and whether an individual is ready to buy at that moment.

To get the answers you need, you have to ask each prospect the right questions at the right times and in the right ways.

This requires skill at asking questions—one of the most powerful ingredients of selling savvy.

FIVE EXCITING BENEFITS TO ASKING QUESTIONS

(1) *Asking questions is the best way to qualify prospects.*

Amateur salespeople waste many valuable hours each day pursuing the wrong customers or talking to people who don't have the authority to make decisions.

Professionals, with a few well-chosen questions, can quickly determine which prospects are prime candidates for sales.

How do they do it?

They organize their qualifying questions by creating a profile of their typical customer. They ask themselves, "What criteria must a person meet to qualify as a bona fide prospect for what I'm selling?"

A list of qualifications might go something like this:

◆ My best prospects live on the west side of town.
◆ They make at least $40,000 a year.
◆ They are between the ages of 25 and 50.
◆ They are married and have children.

Of course, you don't write these down on a sheet of paper, pull it out of your pocket, and check off each criterion as you question your prospects. You fix them firmly in your mind, then ask the questions during your pre-call research to eliminate the people who are not logical prospects.

If you don't find the answers from your research, then you start early in your initial meeting with the prospect to find out all you need to know to determine whether your time can be profitably invested here.

If you're selling a service that has value only to single people, you obviously don't want to spend much time talking to married people.

By asking effective questions, in an inoffensive way, you can target those disqualifying traits up front.

(2) *Asking questions positions you in a consulting role.*

There's that word *positioning* again. The importance of positioning yourself as a consultant instead of a run-of-the-mill salesperson can't be overemphasized.

When you build the sales interview around questions, it's like saying to the prospect, "This interview is about *you;* not about *me.*"

Asking questions helps to build trust and rapport much more effectively than idle chitchat. And if your questions show that you've done your homework and that you know what you are talking about, an interested prospect will start thinking, "Now here's a person who can help me get what I want."

Once the prospect is thinking that way, instead of thinking of you as a pest, you are well on your way to making a sale. All you have to do is keep the right questions coming.

(3) *Questions involve the prospect in the selling process.*

Questions enable you to make the prospect an active participant, not just a disinterested bystander.

Professionals encourage prospects to talk freely by asking them the right questions about their goals, their problems, and their concerns. Then, they sit back and listen to every word each prospect says. Savvy salespeople know that the best way to get people to pay attention to you is to pay attention to them.

Questions also help prospects to focus their own perceptions of their problems. Sometimes, people don't know exactly what the problem is or what they really want, until they have the opportunity to talk it out.

By asking questions, the professional helps prospects define their problems. And, that's the first step toward finding solutions to those problems—solutions that can help you sell your products and services.

(4) *Questions can help you discover and correct misconceptions.*

J.P. Morgan, the great financier, once said "There are always two reasons people do things—the reason they give you and the real reason."

Very often, prospects will refuse to buy or even to see you. They might tell you it's because they don't have the time. But the real reason might be that they're harboring some misconceptions about your company or your products. False notions might have come from one of your competitors. Or they may have arisen from a bad experience with your company many years ago. Or they may have many different sources.

If you can ask the right questions to pin down those false ideas, you can get the process off dead center and move toward closing a sale.

Sometimes, misconceptions can work the other way. It might be you who has the false ideas about a prospect.

For instance, a person might say, "I'll decide and let you know next week." That sounds fair enough, doesn't it?

But what does it mean? That the person you're talking to will have to get approval from someone else? That the prospect is basing the decision on something that might happen next week? Or that you're being told "no" in a roundabout but tactful way?

If you accept the response at face value, it's almost always like kissing the sale good-bye. Ask the right questions. Find the real reason. When questions bring out misconceptions—yours or the prospect's—clear them up and move on toward making the sale.

(5) *Questions enable you to maintain control of the sales interview.*

Intelligently asked questions are like the steering wheel on a car: They give you control. They let you steer the interview in the direction you think it should go, instead of letting it be shoved around by the prospect or by circumstances.

For instance, if your prospect is a big talker, you can shorten the long monologues by asking very pointed questions that pull the interview back on track.

THE DANGERS IN QUESTIONS

Asking questions can be dangerous if you're not careful. Let's look at three big dangers of asking questions in a sales interview— particularly with a new prospect:

(1) *Questions can offend or frighten off the client.*

People sometimes feel manipulated or set up by a salesperson's questions.

One effective method for avoiding this danger is to use softening statements to begin the interview.

For example, you might say, "To make sure I understand your position, do you mind if I ask you a few questions?" or "To be sure I'm not wasting your time, may I ask you a few questions?"

(2) *Questions can lead a talkative person off on tangents.*

Sure, you want to encourage your clients to talk, but the trick is to keep them focused on the main issues of your presentations.

This danger contains its own solution. The real pros become so good at it that the talkative prospect never notices what's happening.

The key is to use the prospect's comments to steer the conversation back to the main issue. Suppose, for example, that you're selling alarm systems and your prospect is rambling on about the family pictures hanging on the wall. You can bring the interview back on track by saying, "I can see that your family is important to you. Wouldn't you feel better if you knew your home was secure?"

If you're a savvy salesperson, you can direct the answer to that question right into a close.

(3) *Questions can reinforce negative feelings.*

Set a pessimist off with a question about the economy and you may generate enough gloom and doom to smother any prospect for a sale.

Questions that lead prospects to talk about deeply personal problems, or about politics, religion, or race can involve them so deeply in those volatile subjects that it may be hard to steer the sales interview back to a positive track. For best results, avoid such issues.

The dangers of asking questions can be avoided. And when questions are skillfully asked, they can become a tremendous aid in selling.

Questions That Yield Information and Involvement

How do you ask questions to get valuable information and involve your prospect in the selling process? There are, indeed, some guidelines that top-flight salespeople in all fields have thoroughly tested and proved effective. Let's take a look:

(1) *Start with broad questions and move toward more narrow questions.*

Open-ended questions—questions that don't narrow the answers down to one or two choices—are less threatening at the beginning of an interview, when the bond of trust has not yet been fully established. Your objective should be to make prospects comfortable by inviting them to share their ideas and information with you.

An interior decorator might say to a prospect, "Can you tell me a little about your decorating motif?" That can be a very productive way to start the interview.

The customer might say, "It follows a Mediterranean theme and the dominant color is tangerine. I love the color and theme, but I'm not sure what to do about the accents."

You've just learned that the prospect likes a Mediterranean motif and is fond of bright colors. You have some valuable clues to use in your sales approach.

But suppose the prospect says, "The present walls are a hideous yellow, and the carpet is orange. The furnishings are that heavy Mediterranean style."

Now you have some clues as to what your prospect *doesn't* like. You can direct your thoughts now toward more subdued colors and lighter furnishings.

As confidence builds, and the sales interview takes on direction, move toward closed questions such as, "Do you think a day bed would go nicely in your sun room?"

Closed questions that focus on specific choices help lead the interview toward the close.

(2) *Ask, then be quiet and listen.*

The prospect can't talk while you're talking. And you don't learn while you're talking.

When you ask questions without waiting for a response, you miss out on information that could help you make the sale. You also irritate the prospect.

While the prospect is talking, amateur salespeople often use the time to decide what to say next. Savvy pros know that's the way sales are lost. They listen to every word prospects say and use the knowledge gained to move them toward closure.

(3) *Keep questions simple and focused.*

Use one idea at a time. Pursue each topic to its logical conclusion. Target your questions. Let each question build on the one before.

If you're selling computers, you might ask, "Do you expect to use this computer mainly for inventory control or for word processing?"

If the answer is "word processing," you might build on that question: "Will you be doing any desktop publishing?"

Followed by "What kind of graphics capabilities do you need?"

By keeping your questions simple and progressive, you gradually build up a picture of what the prospect needs and wants. Armed with that knowledge, you know what product to recommend to meet those needs and wants. Every question the professional asks moves the sales interview closer to the sale.

(4) *Always ask sensitive questions in a non-threatening way.*

Don't ask "How much can you afford to pay for a car?" That question forewarns prospects that you're going to expect them to stretch their budgets to the limit to make the purchase. It's asking, in effect, "are you well-heeled or financially on the ropes?"

The sensitive question is: "How much were you planning to invest in a car?"

When you put the question that way, you're flattering, not threatening the prospect. You're saying, in effect, "I'm aware that you may be able to buy anything on the lot, but I expect that you have some sensible priorities, and I want to help you follow those priorities."

Explain why you must ask a sensitive question. People will answer even touchy questions if they understand why they are asked. For instance, you might say, "To help me recommend the product best suited to your needs, I'd like to ask a few questions about your lifestyle."

(5) *Always ask questions that are easy to answer favorably.*

People would rather answer a question positively than to voice their objections. As you observe your prospects and listen to their comments, you can sense their moods. As you do this, you can ask a series of questions that can be answered "yes," or at least in agreement.

For instance, if you're trying to sell an older home to a young couple, you wouldn't start by asking "Are you willing to invest $30,000 on top of the sales price to bring this place up to modern levels of comfort and convenience?"

Instead, you might start by asking, "Can you picture this house with a balcony outside the master bedroom and a deck off the kitchen?"

"Can you see an island in the middle of that huge kitchen and new oak cabinets where those old metal cabinets are?"

"Wouldn't that small bedroom next to the master bedroom make a gorgeous master bath, maybe with a whirlpool tub in addition to the shower?"

"With a few modernizing touches, this house would be more comfortable and sturdy than houses in that new subdivision that cost $40,000 more. And you wouldn't have to wait for the trees to grow in the front yard and for the garden to be planted and landscaped. If you could get it the way you want it with a total investment that is $10,000 under the price of those newly built homes, would you be interested in buying this one?"

Make it as easy as possible for your prospect to say yes. The secret lies in asking the right questions.

(6) *Turn the statements your prospect makes into questions to clarify or reinforce feelings.*

For example, you might say:

"So Tuesday would be best for you, is that right?" With that question, you have clarified the day the customer seems to prefer.

When a prospect expresses a strong feeling, reinforce it with a question. For example, "Your concern is that your clients don't have time to fill out long forms—is that correct?"

That lets your customer know that you really understood what was said and gives an opportunity for elaboration.

(7) *Use questions to develop presentations.*

For instance, "You mentioned that your present car needs repair. What kinds of repairs does it need?" That question sets the stage for explaining the advantages of a new car.

(8) *Use caution when leading clients with questions.*

Professional buyers and many consumers have become sophisticated enough to realize when they are being set up for the kill, and often they will resent it.

When you say, "If I can get you the right model in the right color at the right price, are you ready to buy today?" most prospects know you're trying to get a commitment before you've even explained the product and will resent this effort to box them in.

Always respect the intelligence of your prospect.

(9) *Use questions to give information.*

It is amazing how much information can be conveyed, and how many opinions can be expressed, through questions.

You might say, "Were you aware that the part you ordered for your machine last month can be adapted to the new system we're introducing next month?"

That question lets you explain that when it's time to upgrade the company's existing system, the logical source for the new equipment will be your company.

(10) *Maintain a confident attitude as you ask questions.*

Your confidence reinforces your positioning as a consultant and builds your prospects' respect for you. People don't mind answering questions asked by a confident professional.

The savvy salesperson realizes the value of becoming a master at the art of asking questions.

Remember: People love to hear themselves talk. If you provide them with that opportunity by asking questions, they'll help you make sales.

CHECK YOUR SELLING SAVVY

I. List five customer-centered questions professional salespeople ask themselves:

    (1) _____

    (2) _____

    (3) _____

    (4) _____

    (5) _____

II. List three customer-centered questions professional salespeople ask their prospects:

    (1) _____

    (2) _____

    (3) _____

III. List five positive things questions can do for the salesperson:

    (1) _____

    (2) _____

    (3) _____

    (4) _____

    (5) _____

IV. List three dangers to be avoided in asking questions:

    (1) _____

    (2) _____

    (3) _____

V. List ten guidelines for asking questions that get prospects involved and produce valuable information for the salesperson:

    (1) _____

    (2) _____

    (3) _____

    (4) _____

    (5) _____

    (6) _____

    (7) _____

    (8) _____

    (9) _____

    (10) _____

Focusing Your
Selling Powers

Focus is the key to turning energy into power.

Water tumbling over a waterfall is energy. But it's only when you direct it through a specific channel that it can turn a dynamo and generate electricity.

Steam rising from a boiling pot is energy. But it's only when you focus it that it can drive locomotives and turn the wheels of industry.

Your sales efforts can be as futile as water over a waterfall or steam from a boiling pot if they're unfocused. Unless you achieve focus, you'll expend plenty of energy, but very little of it will be converted into the power to sell.

To focus steam or falling water so as to harness its power, you have to prepare a channel and direct it through that channel. It works that way with sales efforts too.

Preparation Marks the Professional

In sales, as in any calling, the mark of a professional is preparation.

Competent doctors study their patients' charts carefully before prescribing medication, and they spend considerable time keeping abreast of the latest treatments for diseases.

Lawyers have to be thoroughly grounded in the law, but they also have to prepare carefully for each individual case. You wouldn't want to be represented in court by a lawyer who makes a habit of winging it.

Even professional athletes have to be prepared. They have to know what to expect from the opposing team, and they have to go into each contest with a thoroughly worked-out game plan.

In the boxing ring, it's not the fighter who throws the most hard punches who wins. The victor is the fighter who knows how to direct his punches for maximum impact. Unfocused punches get you nowhere but against the ropes.

Sales pros, too, must be prepared and focused.

One successful salesperson claims that it's ten times harder to build a powerful sales presentation—one that really sells—than it is to prepare a brief to be presented before a supreme court.

He should know. Before he went into sales, he was a trial lawyer in the U.S. Army. He tried 150 cases, including several before the U.S. Court of Military Appeals and its four boards of review.

Professional salespeople know that selling savvy is not simply a matter of instinctively knowing what to say and do when they get in front of prospects. It's being prepared, through research, planning, and practice, to say and do precisely the right things.

THE STRATEGIC AND TACTICAL DIMENSIONS

Let's look at preparation in two dimensions—the strategic and the tactical.

The strategic dimension takes in the big picture. The tactical dimension focuses in on the details.

The difference between strategy and tactics can be appreciated by looking at the way they're applied in military campaigns.

Military strategy is determined with the big picture in mind. During World War II, for instance, the Allied leaders had to determine whether to concentrate their greater efforts on defeating Japan or Germany; whether to strike the Germans first from the South, through Italy, or the west, through France.

In Desert Storm, the United States had to decide whether to launch an immediate ground attack or destroy as much of the enemy as possible from the air.

These were strategic decisions. They determined the overall direction of the battles.

But to implement these strategies, specific plans had to be made. Someone had to decide which beaches to hit in Normandy, which targets were to be bombed, which areas were to be strafed, and where the paratroopers were to be landed. Well in advance of the landings, somebody had to provide for the ships, the aircraft, the landing craft, the guns, and the ammunition. These are tactics.

There's a military axiom that once the troops have hit the beaches, the generals can throw all the books away. The success of the battle now depends upon the tactics on the scene, not the grand strategy crafted from afar.

Sales Strategy and Tactics

Your sales efforts follow the same pattern. You must devise a grand strategy to establish the general framework of your efforts. If you're targeting the wrong businesses with the wrong products, your most brilliant on-the-scene tactics won't work. But if you fumble and stumble over the specifics when it's time for a presentation, your most brilliant strategy will come to naught.

Note that there must be a connection between the general and the specific; between strategies and tactics. The Normandy invasion would have failed had the transports arrived at the hostile shore only to find that no landing craft were on board; had the troops hit the beaches only to find that their weapons wouldn't fire; had they not decided in advance how they would break through all the obstacles the Nazi army had placed on the beaches; and had they not worked out the tactics for taking out the enemy's fortified positions.

Strategic Decisions

The experienced salesperson likewise devises specific tactics with the overall strategy in mind.

You must decide first who your customers will be. If you're selling in-ground swimming pools, you won't waste your time calling on people in rental housing. You know that they're not going to make a major investment in property they're only renting.

If you're selling aluminum siding, you know that you'll make more sales in neighborhoods of modest wood-frame homes than in upscale neighborhoods of all-brick homes.

Next, you must decide on strategies for identifying your potential customers. Will you scout your territory for likely neighborhoods, then go knocking on doors?, Will you mine the telephone directory for prospects, making random calls on names in the white pages?, or Will you search the yellow pages for businesses that might need what you're selling?, Will you make use of Chamber of Commerce directories, Standard and Poor's ratings, and other published sources?, Will you scan the advertising sections of your local newspaper for businesses that might buy your product?, or Will you use the Internet and other on-line resources? These are strategic decisions.

When you've identified the most likely prospects and have devised the most effective avenue for reaching them, you have a focused strategy. But, to return to the military analogy, you've just put the troops ashore. Now, everything depends on your tactics.

Tactical Decisions

After you've identified your individual customers, you'll need to decide what approaches you will use to obtain appointments, and what you'll do and say when it's time for the individual presentation. These are tactical decisions.

Your individual presentation is the key element in your sales tactics. It should get a large share of your attention. In fact, focusing your presentation requires that you do some strategic and some tactical planning.

To examine the strategic dimension, you need to stand back and take an overall look at your whole presentation. What is its purpose? What conditions will be working for and against your success? What must you do to make a sale? That's the overall, strategic dimension.

Studying this dimension will enable you to plan the major points of the presentation. You can decide whom the presentation is for, what the prospect's main areas of interest are, where and when you will meet, and other broad matters.

These decisions will give you a general framework within which to work out the details. The experienced professional leaves none of the little details to chance.

If you walk out of a presentation only to realize that you've forgotten to get your customer's credit card number, you're not focusing on the tactical dimensions of that sale. And forgetting that kind of detail can cancel all the effects of the most powerful presentation in history.

A dynamic presentation is just as ineffective as a mediocre presentation if the end result is the same—no sale.

Your tactics must have a direct connection with your strategy.

For example, your strategy may call for the use of testimonial letters during your presentation to build the prospect's confidence in the product. But if you have to fumble and search through a jumble of unorganized papers to pull out the testimonial letter, you may find yourself facing a yawning prospect. And if the testimonials are dog-eared and tattered, what kind of confidence are you building?

The use of testimonial letters is a strategy. Their organization and appearance is a tactic. Your strategy can be a good one, but if your tactics fail, you're like troops landing on a hostile beach with wet ammo. Don't get caught in that disastrous situation.

By thinking about both strategy and tactics—the general and the specific, the big items and the small ones, the macro and the micro—the professional salesperson makes sure that all selling activities are working together to move the prospect toward a buying decision. Not a single detail is overlooked.

WHAT PLANNING CAN DO FOR YOUR PRESENTATION

If you're like most salespeople, you might be thinking, "I know I should do a better job of preparing." You're probably right, and here are some powerful reasons for giving careful attention to the planning of your preparation:

(1) *Planning helps you focus on all the value you are creating for your customers.*

You, your company, and your products are no better than your most marginal competitor unless you have the ability and the know-how to sell and interpret the differences.

When you work to build value for your customer, you end up selling to yourself as well. You are able to see all the value you are creating, and you become convinced that your price is a solid value to the prospect. That conviction is vital to successful selling. If you don't believe your product is worth what your company charges for it, you'll have a tough time convincing a prospect.

The more you know about a product or service, the greater your ability to sell its quality and benefits to the prospect.

You must know your product to interpret and sell its differential advantages over competing products. Preparing helps you to understand how great the product is.

(2) *Preparing your presentation enables you to relax.*

You can't give your best presentation while you're worried about what vital point you might be leaving out. If you're thoroughly prepared in advance, you won't be worried about what you're forgetting. You can concentrate fully on giving the most dynamic presentation you're capable of giving.

Preparing is the only way to develop the kind of confidence that will inspire trust in your prospect. As you plan out every detail of the presentation, you can feel your confidence level rising.

If you rely solely on your instincts for making a presentation, you risk forgetting some of your most persuasive material.

Remember: The more confidence you have in yourself, the more confidence the prospect will have in you.

If you are familiar with all the elements of your presentation, you will be comfortable when talking with a prospect. Questions and objections won't throw you off balance.

(3) *Preparing your presentation saves time.*

When you're properly prepared, you can cover every detail in much less time than when you're shooting from the hip.

As a result, you don't waste your time or the prospect's time, trying to organize your thoughts and get everything in.

In most cases, you have only a certain amount of time to get your point across to your prospects. Fumbling for facts or figures burns up that valuable time.

A well-planned presentation helps you make smooth transitions from one point to another and move the interview steadily toward its logical conclusion—making the sale and getting the order.

(4) *A planned presentation makes you look like a pro.*

A well-organized sales presentation says to the prospect, "Here is a well-organized person who handles business efficiently and effectively." That's the kind of person buyers want to do business with. A strong presentation demonstrates that prospects can trust you to handle all the important details for them.

As your prospects listen to your presentations, they'll be asking themselves:

◆ Can I use this product?
◆ Can I rely on this salesperson and company?
◆ What's the difference in this sales pitch and all the others I've heard over the years?

- ◆ Does this salesperson really understand my problems?
- ◆ Can I rely on these recommendations?
- ◆ Can I justify spending that much money on this product, right now?

The more of those questions you answer satisfactorily, the better your chances for making a sale.

To be able to answer all those questions, you must have your act together when it's time to perform.

SIX POINTERS FOR MAXIMUM IMPACT

How can you prepare to make an effective presentation every time you have the opportunity?

The secret lies in focusing every detail of the presentation. Let's look a little more closely at how savvy salespeople focus their energies on building powerful presentations.

Here are six proven ideas to help you focus for maximum impact and prepare for outstanding client relationships:

(1) *Focus on your objectives.*

Obviously, you can't get anywhere if you don't know where you're going. When you prepare your presentation, you're going for a sale. Everything you do or say must be targeted toward that objective. Every element of a powerful presentation is crafted to persuade the prospect to buy what you're selling.

But along the way to that major goal are many interim objectives. First, you want to get the prospect's attention. Without it, your efforts are futile. You want to make sure your prospect understands what we're selling. And you want to get across the most crucial benefits for that particular prospect.

As you're preparing your presentation, ask yourself this question: "What will move the prospect closer to a decision to buy?"

When it comes to deciding what to include in your presentation and what to leave out, ask yourself: "How will this affect my goal? Will it lead the prospect to buy, or lead to a rejection of my offer?"

(2) *Focus on the prospect.*

Learn everything you can about each of your prospects before you plan your presentations.

For every prospect, ask yourself:

◆ What does this person need or want that I can provide?
◆ How can I help this prospect meet those needs and desires?
◆ What is this individual's business or position within a business?
◆ How will this bit of information affect the way I make my presentation?
◆ What benefits will most impress this prospect?

By asking such questions, you're focusing on the factors that will make that prospect want to buy from you.

So gather all the information you can possibly obtain. Then, you can custom-design each presentation for an individual prospect.

There's awesome power in personalizing each presentation.

The world is made up of two kinds of people: those who walk into a room and say, "Here I am," and those who walk in and say, "Ah, there you are!"

The salesperson who says, "Ah, there you are" is the one who gets the business.

Psychologists tell us that one of the most basic of human cravings is to feel important. Custom-designing your presentations makes your prospects feel important. You're going to the time and trouble to do something just for them.

Tailoring sales interviews to individual prospects is selling savvy of the finest kind. Remember that peddlers sell products and services; professionals sell people—one customer at a time.

(3) *Focus on the content of your presentation.*

What's the main message you want to get across to your prospect?

If you're like most salespeople, you have volumes of material and information on the products or services you sell. You could talk for three days straight and almost never repeat yourself.

But prospects don't have time for that. And even if they did have the time, they wouldn't want to be bored with all the minute features of your products.

They have one essential question: "What's in it for me?"

To create powerful presentations, you need to determine for each prospect what benefits will have the greatest impact. What you might include in one presentation you wouldn't necessarily include in another.

For example, let's say you sell boats. One prospect is looking for a fishing boat. In that case, you would include all the information you have on fishing boats—which ones have trolling motors, fresh-fish storage, bait holders, depth-finders, and so on.

Those are the features that a fishing enthusiast would find exciting. They are related to the fisher's needs and desires.

But if a family is looking for a boat they can use for water skiing and general recreation, you'd talk to them about power, passenger capacity, speed, and handling.

There would be a tremendous difference between the needs of the water-skiing family and those of the fishing enthusiast.

Focusing the content of a presentation can be broken into two steps:

♦ *Make a list of everything necessary to sell the prospect.*

Include all the basics, such as price, financing terms, and delivery arrangements.

♦ *Using the information you have collected, form a list of the special features that appeal uniquely to that individual prospect.*

The more your presentations focus on individual prospects, the more impact they will carry.

(4) *Focus on organization.*

Organize the presentation by connecting all the parts so that they flow in a logical sequence. A presentation that jumps from topic to topic, with no sense of direction, can be very confusing to a prospect.

For example, if you talk about terms and delivery schedules before you demonstrate a product, you're answering questions the prospect is not yet asking. Not only will it be confusing, but it will also waste a lot of time. You'll probably have to repeat all that information when the prospect is ready to hear it.

The professional makes sure all the parts of a presentation work together to create one smooth performance.

(5) *Focus on clarity.*

Make sure people understand what you are telling them. That means to keep things simple.

The best way to do this is to write out everything you hope to cover in your presentation. Then, start cutting and editing to get clean, concise language that says precisely what you want the prospect to hear.

Use strong selling words, and avoid big words and jargon. These often sound pretentious and can confuse your prospects.

Prospects want straight facts and helpful information in easily understood language.

The salesperson in a highly specialized field must use extra caution in this area. It's easy to get caught up in high-tech jargon and completely overlook the simple benefits most likely to appeal to a prospect. If you're using technical language your prospect doesn't understand, you might as well be giving your presentation in ancient Greek. Remember: Keep it simple; make it clear.

(6) *Focus on application.*

Sometimes, the best ideas in theory fall flat in reality.

Make sure your presentations actually convey the message you are trying to send. The best way to do this is to have a "dress rehearsal." Ask a friend or colleague to critique your presentation.

If you notice that a particular word, phrase, or part of the presentation seems dead, re-examine it and make adjustments.

Practice for High-Impact Presentations

Although these six ideas can help you build a powerful presentation, there is no substitute for practice. Once you're comfortably sure that your presentation is ready, start practicing to get yourself ready.

Selling savvy comes only with constant drilling on your well-organized presentation. As we've seen before, the basics of selling are second nature to professional salespeople. And one of those basics is making high-impact presentations.

Many amateur salespeople use the excuse that "canned" presentations detract from the impact of their interviews. That's a cop-out that's costing thousands of salespeople a lot of money.

The secret is to practice the presentation so well that you can give it in a spontaneous way.

After you've rehearsed the material before a colleague, keep going over it in your mind. On your way to call on a prospect, imagine yourself giving the presentation. Imagine what the prospect will say, and how you will respond. This mental rehearsal will prepare you for the actual situation and you'll be more comfortable when you're actually giving the presentation and fielding the objections.

Familiarity Breeds Performance

Selling savvy is more than instinct. It comes from knowing your material—your product and your individual prospects—so well that you can perform the presentation in your sleep.

Professional salespeople understand this.

I'm not suggesting that you sit down in front of a prospect and recite your presentation word for word.

But if you want to be sure you will remember everything you want to tell your prospect, you need to be so familiar with your material that you can run through a mental checklist as you cover each point.

Being that confident with your material will free you to focus all your energy on the sales interview. So, practice, practice, practice!

Here's a tip on making your practice time even more effective: Rehearse your presentation with enthusiasm—the same level of enthusiasm you would use if you were actually giving the presentation.

Enthusiastic practice will enable you to give an enthusiastic presentation. And enthusiasm is one of the greatest assets a salesperson can cultivate.

Work on Your Attitude

It doesn't matter how many times you've called on a prospect. Every time you walk in, you need to be ready to do your best performance.

So once you are thoroughly familiar with your presentation, work on your attitude.

I learned a long time ago that if I am not enthusiastic about what I'm saying, it is impossible to get anyone else enthusiastic about it.

Developing selling savvy comes from work; it comes from experience. Planning and preparing your presentations is a major part of that process.

To be more successful as a professional salesperson, increase your selling savvy by focusing all your energies for maximum impact. Go into each presentation with a full head of steam. But make sure it's focused for maximum power.

CHECK YOUR SELLING SAVVY

I. List some strategic decisions you have to make in your sales career:

    (1) _____

    (2) _____

    (3) _____

    (4) _____

    (5) _____

II. List some tactical decisions you have to make:

    (1) _____

    (2) _____

    (3) _____

    (4) _____

    (5) _____

III. How do your tactical decisions relate to your strategic decisions?

_____

_____

_____

IV. List four things a well-planned presentation can do for you:

    (1) _____

    (2) _____

    (3) _____

    (4) _____

V. List six ideas that will help you focus for maximum impact:

(1) _____

(2) _____

(3) _____

(4) _____

(5) _____

(6) _____

10

Presentations With Power to Sell

The sales presentation is where your selling savvy comes to its moment of truth. All else is preliminary. This is where your sale is made or lost. It's also where the amateurs are separated from the pros.

You can usually identify the amateurs by the false assumptions they carry into the presentation. The two most common are the *fatalistic* and the *invincibility* assumptions.

Amateurs with the *fatalistic* assumption go in with the idea that the sale is up to the prospect. If prospects like their products, they'll buy them, they reason. If they don't, they won't. And since a certain percentage of prospects will like their products, all they have to do is play the numbers game: Make enough calls and you'll make your sale. Why spend a lot of time polishing your presentation and tailoring it to the individuals you're trying to sell? Just keep moving on till somebody says yes.

Salespeople with the *invincibility* assumption have the opposite attitude: They approach each prospect with the smug confidence that the sale is already made.

"I'm the greatest salesperson in the world," such people say. "I can sell anybody. Nobody can resist my pitch."

It's all right to have a positive attitude. In fact, a positive attitude is a powerful piece of sales equipment. But you also have to touch base with reality. And the reality is that you're not invincible and there are plenty of people out there in Salesland who will find it quite easy to say no to you.

The flaw in the invincibility assumption is that it reflects a self focus rather than a customer focus. It puts the emphasis on the salesperson's charm and persuasive powers and not on the prospect's needs and wants.

Moving the Prospect Off Dead Center

The real pros make neither assumption. They know that they're not going to make a sale on every call. But they know that every call is a potential sale and that the percentage of successful calls will rise in proportion to the skill and effort they put into their presentations. They see each prospect as sitting on dead center, squarely between a yes and a no, and they take it as their challenge to shift the balance to the yes side. Knowing that no sale has been made until the order has been signed, they look for ways to move the prospect to a buying decision.

SALES PRESENTATIONS WITH MOVING POWER

To get that movement, they:

- Help the prospect discover a pressing need or overpowering desire.
- Convince the prospect that what they're selling will meet that need or desire better than anything else available.
- Build enough value to outweigh the cost.
- Give the prospect a compelling reason to act immediately.

Moving your prospect to a buying decision is a formidable challenge. You have only a limited time available to accomplish the sale. You have competitors out there with similar products, eager to snatch your goods out of the prospect's hands and replace them with their own. Add to that the normal tension of the selling situation, and it becomes clear: This is no game for amateurs. To get that sale, you need a powerful sales presentation delivered with a lot of selling savvy.

Making powerful presentations to qualified people is the way professionals persuade enough prospects to buy their products at a profit.

Put Prospects in Prime Time

Top salespeople manage their schedules to allow them to spend most of their prime time in front of prospects. They prepare thoroughly to take maximum advantage of their opportunities to sell and use every presentation as an opportunity to learn. They learn what strategies make their presentations powerful; and they learn what strategies are ineffective.

Develop a Potent Selling System

A powerful presentation, by my definition, is a systematic process that consistently produces sales. If you really want to succeed in this business, you have to develop an effective selling system—one that works consistently for you. And you have to use that system over and over, until you get so good that it fits you, your product, and your customers like a custom-tailored suit.

That's basic. Just as using a saw and hammer becomes second nature to a carpenter; just as the choice of paint brushes, the blending of colors, and the elements of composition become second nature to an artist, so the crafting and delivery of a presentation must become second nature to a salesperson. You're not selling with savvy until you can make your presentation without consciously thinking about what you're doing.

Powerful Presentations Are Propelling Processes

Notice that I defined a powerful presentation as a process, not an event—or even a series of events. A process is dynamic. An event is static. A process is continuous action. A series of events is intermittent action. The difference between a process and an event is like the difference between an oar and a propeller. With the oar, you move stroke by stroke. With the propeller, you're constantly powering toward your objective.

Amateurs like to break the presentation down into a series of events. First comes the greeting. Next comes the warm-up. Then, they qualify the prospect, demonstrate the product, handle objections, handle more objections, and—if luck is with them—close the sale. With each event, they pull on the oars, then pause for the next stroke.

In contrast, the pros are always warming up their prospects. They are always qualifying. They're asking for commitments from the moment they begin. They don't wait until the objection-handling stage; when objections arise, they deal with them immediately. The propeller is always in motion. The process is always in progress.

Watch a skilled veteran guide the selling process. It's like a magnificent symphony. It has rhythm, tonal variations, recurring motifs, and balance.

One set of instruments is playing at one moment, and a totally different set at another, but the effect is totally harmonious. And when it's finished, the only natural thing to do is wrap up the sale and walk out with the order.

When you can do that, and do it consistently and superbly, you have selling savvy—and an incredibly prosperous future.

FOUR PROVEN STRATEGIES FOR POWERFUL PRESENTATIONS

How can you develop such a system for making powerful presentations? Here are four strategies that can help you master a systematic process for consistently producing sales:

(1) *Keep the prospect involved.*

Make your presentation customer-centered, not product-centered.

We've made the point before, but it bears repeating: The greatest secret to success in selling is to help people get what they want.

Selling begins the moment you have the prospect's full attention; and it ends the moment you lose the prospect's full attention. The more involved the prospect becomes, the greater your chances of making a sale.

BUILD YOUR PRESENTATION AROUND QUESTIONS

One effective way to lead people to what they want is to build the whole presentation around questions.

Salespeople who don't ask a lot of questions during every sales interview are not making presentations; they're putting on performances. There's a big difference.

Obviously, you need to ask questions to obtain information about what you should do next.

But the real value of the probing approach to selling is that it helps prospects discover what they want, and it guides them toward the conclusion that buying your product is the best way to get it.

Using questions to involve the prospect gets rid of the adversarial relationship that can turn a presentation into an argument; a contest of one-upmanship. Instead of pitting salesperson against prospect, the selling process becomes one in which two people are searching for ways to work together for mutual benefits.

Powerful Presentations Transfer Psychological Ownership

A powerful presentation is a gradual transfer of psychological ownership. When you walk in, the product is yours. The more involved the prospect becomes, the more the ownership shifts.

The moment the prospect begins to think "That's my product," the sale is made. From then on, it's just a matter of working out the details.

That kind of mental transfer of ownership doesn't happen abruptly; it's a gradual process that must be deliberately orchestrated by a skilled salesperson. Nothing helps you to move the process along more effectively than asking the right questions at the right times.

Customize for Specific Needs and Concerns

Another good technique for involving the prospect is to customize every presentation for the specific needs and concerns of the one or two people before you.

Of course, it's important to memorize standard benefit statements, feature demonstrations, and other basic components that you use repeatedly. It's the only way you can present them with power.

But it's a little like selling a suit of clothes. You have certain styles you show to sedate businesspeople, other styles for flamboyant entertainers; some for young swingers, others for older professionals. You suit the style to the customer.

Once your customer decides on a suit, you can tailor it precisely to the individual's shape and dimensions.

How to Size Up a Prospect

From the moment you walk in to make a presentation, you are sizing up the prospect.

You look for clues to personality type, buying style, decision-making process, motivations, problems, interests—anything and everything to help custom-fit your presentation to the unique person you're talking with.

For example, if the prospect talks in terms of feelings and emotions, you structure your presentation around feelings and emotions. If you're dealing with a no-nonsense, facts-oriented person, you get to the bottom line as quickly as possible.

If the prospect likes to be part of the crowd, focus on the many people who own your product. If you're dealing with a free-spirited individualist, show how the product can separate its owner from the crowd. If the prospect seems to be driven by fear and anxiety, look for ways your product can relieve the fears and anxieties.

Build Around the Benefits Your Prospect Likes

Most of all, build your presentation around the specific benefits the prospect finds most attractive. As your probing questions reveal insights about the prospect, adapt your presentation to fit what you learn.

Here, it's important to note two very crucial issues:

◆ *You have to monitor prospects constantly to stay abreast of whatever is going through their minds.*

Is the prospect losing interest or doubting something you've said? Are you getting outside interference?

Savvy salespeople stay alert for every signal that might give them a glimpse into what the prospect is thinking.

They don't build a presentation on what they *wish* was happening, or even on what they *expect* to happen. They stay on top of what *is* happening and act accordingly.

◆ *You can be free to monitor what the customer is thinking only when you're so well prepared that you can forget about what you are doing.*

Planned versus Canned Presentations

A planned presentation is not a canned presentation. To plan for a presentation, you must consider all the possibilities.

The key is always to know in advance precisely what you will do if certain things happen during a presentation. If you can avoid reacting to surprises, you will be free to adapt to almost anything your customers say and you can keep them involved through every phase of the sales process.

This is where mental rehearsal can be helpful. Envision yourself giving your presentation and encountering a variety of objections. Then, imagine yourself overcoming the objections. Imagine the words and phrases you would use; the body language you would employ. Be hard on yourself in these mental portrayals. In your imagination, create really tough prospects and have them bring up every difficult objection you can think of. Then, decide how you would handle such objections, and imagine yourself responding to them smoothly and effectively.

If you do that, you'll be prepared for such situations when they arise during actual presentations. You'll know exactly how to respond, and you'll do so smoothly and professionally.

(2) *Build credibility and trust.*

Smart salespeople start from the assumption that prospects are suspicious of everything they do and every word they say. They focus their efforts on removing the suspicions and building trust and credibility. Only by building this trust and credibility can they move through the sales cycle.

TECHNIQUES FOR BUILDING TRUST

Here are some techniques for building trust:

◆ *Position yourself as a credible person who deserves to be trusted.*

Professional salespeople reflect credibility in the way they look, talk, and act—the way they package themselves. The savvy salesperson presents an image of credibility and professionalism.

◆ *Be sensitive to a prospect's reaction to everything you say and do.*

Use verbal and non-verbal feedback from prospects to monitor the trust bond you're building. If a prospect demonstrates a favorable response to a particular point or action, stick with it and build on it.

If something you're doing seems to annoy the prospect, abandon it gracefully and move on to a less-threatening topic or technique.

◆ *Don't overload the presentation.*

A prospect can absorb only so much information. So always keep it simple.

Feel Carefully in the Dark

Sometimes, it's difficult to judge which material to use in a presentation with a particular client until the presentation is actually under way. In a sense, you're feeling your way in the dark. When you're doing that, you don't just barrel blindly ahead. You feel your way carefully until you're sure you're on the right path.

So in such situations, professional salespeople don't overwhelm their prospects with a mass of information thrown out at once. Instead, they feed them information a little at a time and watch for reactions.

◆ *Build credibility through sales aids or literature.*

People believe what they see. And when they see information in print, they'll often accept it more readily than they'll accept spoken assurances. But be sure your materials have a professional look about them. Dog-eared, tattered, and blurry materials say "rank amateur" to your prospects and turn them off quickly.

◆ *Back up every claim you make.*

Don't just throw out an uncorroborated statement. It's one thing to say, "This jewel will go from zero to sixty in six seconds." It's another thing to produce an actual published road test with authenticated acceleration figures. It's one thing to say, "She'll get 30 miles to the gallon." Miles-per-gallon boasts rank right down there with fishing tales for credibility. But as Dizzy Dean, the Hall of Fame pitcher and raconteur, used to say, "It ain't bragging if you can do it." If you can show official EPA figures, you're not bragging.

◆ *Emphasize what the product will do for the customer.*

Professional salespeople answer the prospect's ever-present question: "What's in it for me?"

Let's face it: Customers are becoming jaded and cynical. If they've been in business long, they've heard so many sales presentations that they all sound like boring reruns. So impressing your prospects becomes an ever-increasing challenge.

Steer Clear of the Stereotype

What makes it even harder is the public's stereotypical image of the salesperson. Studies consistently show that salespeople rank high on the average person's list of people who can't be trusted. If you want to be trusted as a salesperson, you have to stay as far away from the stereotype as possible. You can't fast-talk your way to trust and credibility. You have to get it the old-fashioned way: by earning it.

(3) *Focus on building value.*

Think of the sales cycle as an old-fashioned set of merchant's scales. On the one side, you have the price. On the other side is the customer's perception of value.

At the beginning of a presentation, the price almost always outweighs the value—at least in the prospect's mind.

The salesperson states the price, but it's the customer who always determines the value. The salesperson's challenge is to build up the value in the customer's mind until it tips the scales and outweighs the price. When that happens, the transfer of ownership is complete.

BUILD THE INTRINSIC VALUE

You may protest at this point that the value of a product is a constant thing. You can't build it and you can't diminish it. If it's not there at the start of your presentation, it won't be there at the end.

You're right if you're talking about *intrinsic* value—the value a commodity possesses in and of itself. But professional salespeople don't just deal with intrinsic value. They deal with *perceived* value.

A piece of canvas covered with oil pigments has a relatively small intrinsic value. But if it bears an authentic Rembrandt signature, its perceived value goes sky-high. And that's the value people use when they buy and sell the canvas.

Two pairs of blue jeans may be cut from the same cloth according to identical styles. Their intrinsic values are the same. But if one has the Calvin Klein signature on the hip and the other doesn't, which one has the greater perceived value?

The most important thing to remember about value is that what counts is always the perceived value—and that's in the customer's mind. The second-most important thing to remember is that the perceived value always has to be raised before the prospect will buy.

Any time you find yourself in a price-haggling contest, you can be sure that product does not yet have enough value for the prospect. In simple terms, the prospect is not yet sold.

How to Build Value to Tip the Scales

How can you build enough value to tip the scales in favor of a sale?

Start by assuming that the prospect does not know the value of your product.

Prospects may say, "I know it's a good product," "I've always enjoyed doing business with your company," or "I've wanted one of these for a long time." But professional salespeople know that these words are not synonymous with "I'm ready to buy from you."

The Myth That "Everybody Knows the Value"

And don't ever believe the myth that "everybody knows the value" of an established product.

I once bought two Mercedes-Benz automobiles from a novice

salesperson who had the selling savvy to open his presentation by asking, "Do you know what's so special about owning a Mercedes?"

When I said I didn't, he proceeded to show me.

To customers, all values are equal until someone points out the differences.

There's a lot of competition out there in the real world where you and I sell. Unless you can clearly focus your product's differential advantage, customers are always going to argue over your prices—or worse yet, buy from your competitors.

Make Them Experience the Value

But there's another technique my Mercedes salesperson used: He made me experience the value of his product.

That young man took me out and put me behind the wheel, so I could actually experience for myself the thrill of owning the product.

At every opportunity during that drive, he pointed out values he thought I might miss. He put me in the driver's seat. He constantly reinforced what I was experiencing by explanations and repetition. And finally, he used another highly effective technique for building value: He asked questions to make sure I understood and believed what he was showing and telling me.

When you can get a prospect to feed back your strongest benefits to you, you're well on your way to closing the sale.

Remember this strategy: Always focus on building value where it counts most—in the customer's mind. If building value doesn't work, build more value. That's selling savvy.

(4) *Take charge and stay in charge of the selling process.*

People don't just buy; they have to be sold.

That doesn't mean that they want to be pressured or abused or manipulated into buying something they don't want or need.

But they do expect to be sold. In fact, most people actually enjoy seeing a master salesperson put on a thoroughly professional presentation—especially if they already have some desire for the product.

To take charge, you first have to come alive. Enthusiasm sells. Entertaining presentations sell. Get excited about what you are doing. It's the best way to get other people excited.

HERE'S HOW TO TAKE CHARGE

◆ *Come alive.*

You can no more get a prospect enthusiastic without being enthusiastic yourself than you can come back from a place you haven't been.

Sell yourself first; then you can sell the prospect.

Let your enthusiasm show. Be animated. Move around. Be fun to watch. The more you're into what you're doing, the more you can get your prospects into it.

◆ *Position yourself as an expert.*

Know what you are talking about, then prove to the prospect that you know.

◆ *Use powerful selling words.*

Poet Ralph Waldo Emerson said, "Say what you think in words as strong as cannonballs." When it comes to selling, that's good advice.

Build a vocabulary of strong selling words—words such as *proven, effective, results, value, researched, action,* and *agreement.*

Avoid words that unsell—words such as: *bargain, deal, steal, contract,* and *sign here.*

What do you think of when you hear the word *bargain*? A basement full of cheap goods? When somebody says *deal,* we often think of something shady. A *steal* is something illegal, unless you're on a baseball diamond.

The difference between a *contract* and an *agreement* is that agreements signify mutual accord; contracts signify unbreakable commitments. Agreements are friendly and personal; contracts are cold and impersonal. When you ask a prospect to "okay this agreement," you're asking for an affirmation that "This is what we agreed to." When you say "If you'll just sign this contract . . ." or "Just sign on the dotted line," you're saying, "Once I have your John Hancock, there's no backing out."

Think about the words you use most often in your presentations. Do they turn prospects on or turn them off?

Professional salespeople master vocabularies of strong selling words and use them with great power.

◆ *Develop a good sense of timing.*

It's up to the salesperson to keep the selling process moving at a steady and productive pace. Yet, you have to be careful that you never move too fast for the customer. A major part of selling savvy is knowing whether it's time to move in, to move out, or to move on.

Professionals realize that a presentation is more than a performance. They're not just there to entertain or even to persuade. They're there to sell products and services.

Even the most dynamic presentations are meaningless if they don't eventually lead to sales.

So follow the four major strategies outlined in this chapter. Develop and master powerful presentations, which consistently produce sales for you.

That's selling savvy.

CHECK YOUR SELLING SAVVY

I. What are the two most common mistaken assumptions that amateurs take into the sales process?

(1) _____

(2) _____

II. List four techniques the pros use to move the prospect off dead center:

(1) _____

(2) _____

(3) _____

(4) _____

III. List four proven strategies for mastering a systematic sales process:

(1) _____

(2) _____

(3) _____

(4) _____

IV. What two crucial issues should you keep in mind as you involve the prospect in the presentation?

(1) _____

(2) _____

V. List six techniques for building credibility and trust:

(1) _____

(2) _____

(3) _____

(4) _____

(5) _____

(6) _____

VI. What is the difference between intrinsic value and perceived value, and why should salespeople emphasize the latter?

_____

_____

_____

_____

_____

_____

VII. List four tips for taking charge of the selling process:

(1) _____

(2) _____

(3) _____

(4) _____

11

How to Turn Objections Into Sales

"No thanks," says the prospect. "I don't want to buy your product."

"Thanks for your time," says the amateur salesperson. "I guess I'll be on my way."

But for the professional, the sales call is far from over. Savvy salespeople know that the first objection doesn't mean "Pack up and leave"; it means "Time to go to work."

Professionals recognize the word "no," as a signal to look for more information. They want to know why a prospect doesn't want to buy. When they know the reasons, they can start eliminating them one by one.

Once you've eliminated the reasons for saying no, you're likely to make your sale. But before you can eliminate them, you must be aware that they exist, and you must know what they are. How do you identify them?

Turn Objections Into Nuggets of Information

Successful salespeople share at least one vital characteristic of selling savvy: They recognize that objections are the surest indicators of the reasons a prospect declines to buy.

The amateur takes the first negative remark as a definite no and closes the interview, not the sale. Some amateurs even take objections as personal rejections. The pros know that the objection is, at worst, a business refusal. But they also know that it may be a request for more information; a sign of interest.

They proceed to determine what information they need to supply to settle the questions in their prospects' minds. Then, they go on and make the sales.

That's how the pros turn objections and stalls into sales. It's called selling savvy.

FOUR REASONS TO BUY

Long ago, I learned that people buy for four basic reasons: fear, pride, gain, and imitation.

Why do you buy fire insurance on your home?

Because you fear that it might burn; so you buy financial protection.

Why do you buy a nice new car instead of tooling around town in a beat-up but reliable old pick-up?

Because your car, in addition to providing basic transportation, is also a status symbol. It's a source of pride.

Why do you invest in an expensive personal computer when you've always gotten along with a manual typewriter and a calculator?

Because a personal computer enables you to do more work faster and gains you access to an almost unlimited supply of information.

Why do you lay out good money for membership in a country club?

Because among your peers it's the thing to do; you imitate the people you respect and want to impress.

Think about all the things you own or want to own. Why do you want them? Your reasons will boil down to one of those four: fear, pride, gain, or imitation.

FOUR REASONS PEOPLE DON'T BUY

People also refuse to buy for four basic reasons. Before we explore ways to identify and settle objections and stalls, it's important that we understand these reasons. They are:

(1) *Lack of confidence.*

The prospect has no confidence in either the salesperson, the product or service, or the company offering the goods.

This reason is, many times, the most difficult one to pin down, and it's even harder to fix. People usually won't come right out and say, "No. The last time I bought from your company I felt cheated," "No. I hear your products are worthless," or "No. I don't think I can trust you." They soft-pedal their concerns with such phrases as, "We're really not interested at this time" or "We don't need anything."

Sometimes, you can flush out the reason with questions: "Have you had any experience with our products? How have they worked for you? What have you heard people say about them? or Do you know anything about our company?" Let the prospect know that you're not fishing for compliments but are genuinely interested in the way your company and its products are perceived.

Unless you can identify lack of confidence as the problem, you won't be able to solve the problem, and you won't close the sale.

When you discover a lack of confidence in the company, it's usually best to ask management for help in finding a solution.

When prospects show lack of confidence in the product or service, it usually means that they don't believe what you're selling will meet their needs.

One way to deal with that objection is to stage a trial demonstration. Another is to get a minimal order so the customer can use the product on a trial basis.

Confidence can sometimes be built through testimonials from satisfied users in similar situations.

(2) *No need for it.*

When customers say they don't need your product or service, they're usually saying that the desire to buy has not been sufficiently stimulated.

Very few prospects in the United States really need what most salespeople are selling. Probably 90% of the things Americans spend money on are luxuries. They need to eat, but do they really need to go to that fancy, up-town restaurant? They need a place to live, but do they really need wall-to-wall carpet, whirlpool baths, and hot tubs on the rear deck?

People rarely buy something because they need it. They buy it because they want it.

What does this tell us about selling? It clearly suggests that when prospects say they don't need the product or service you're selling, you have to build value to help them decide. You have to awaken desires they don't know they have. You may not be able to establish the **need** to move up from a Chevy pick-up to a Cadillac sedan, but you can make Cadillac ownership so attractive that your prospect will be panting for a chance to park one in the garage.

To awaken the thirst, the savvy salesperson resorts to the professional's standard tool: questions. What is it that turns the prospect on?

Super salesperson Frank Bettger's powerful insight will then move you toward the sale: "Once you help people discover what they want, they will move heaven and earth to get it."

(3) *Lack of money.*

People generally will find the money to buy what they really want. So when someone says, "I don't have the money," it usually means "I don't want it badly enough to pay the price."

An item is worth no more than a prospect is willing to pay for it. When prospects say, "The price is too high," amateurs often look for ways to cut the price. Professionals look for ways to enhance the value. They look for new benefits they can highlight for each customer, in addition to the benefits the customer already likes.

Professional salespeople try to convince their prospects that they can't afford *not* to buy their products or services.

When your prospect is convinced that the value is too great to pass up, you can close the sale—time and again, day after day, year after year.

(4) *No hurry.*

Every salesperson is familiar with the prospect who says, "Let me think about it a couple of days."

Such prospects may want someone else to be in on the decision. They may want to wait a while, or they may want to look around some more.

Who Has Authority to Order?

To deal effectively with the delay objection—or the stall—one question must be settled right away: Does the prospect have the authority to give you the order?

You want to know this before you even give your presentation.

If the prospect says, "I'll talk to the decision maker about it," you need to try every way possible to see the decision maker yourself. After all, you're better at selling your product than some underling is who can, at best, repeat what you say. Your go-between is likely to forget most of your selling points and will deliver the rest with a strong dose of personal opinion. This trap will cost you the sale 90% of the time.

How to Overcome the Stall

If, though, you find that the person can buy, try these tactics:

- ◆ Give immediacy to the prospect's actions.
- ◆ Build value, build value, and build value.
- ◆ Make the prospect feel that the deal won't be as good later.

Special "today only" rates or offers can be very effective for expediting a customer's decision.

If you can pin down the dominant reason behind a prospect's refusal to buy, you'll be in a far better position to overcome the problem and close a sale.

Whatever the objection—whatever the basic reason—you cannot make a sale until the key issue is settled.

Think of yourself as a consumer for a minute. When was the last time you bought something that you didn't need, desire, or find valuable?

When was the last time you bought something that you figured you could get for less at a later time or from some other supplier? When was the last time you bought something from a person you didn't trust?

Selling savvy is pinpointing those types of objections, then building on the true motivations of the prospect.

Understand the Objections

The most important step in handling objections is to understand them.

When you encounter a prospect who has appeared interested in your presentation and your product but hesitates to buy, it's vital that you ask enough probing questions to uncover the real reason for the hesitancy.

Some prospects become masters at throwing up smoke screens. They'll give you five reasons why they don't want to buy today. But when you look carefully, all the reasons are the same.

Defining a prospect's real objection is often the toughest part of closing the sale. The actual reasons are often concealed so well that it takes real savvy to ferret them out.

For example, a prospect might say, "We're very happy with our present supplier." The hidden message might be "I hate your company's credit manager."

Until the real objection is pinpointed, you're wasting your time in talking about the superiority of your products or services, the advantages you can offer over the present supplier, or any other benefits you might bring up.

HOW TO TELL WHEN AN OBJECTION IS REAL

How do you know when an objection is real, and when it's just a smoke screen to cover up a deeper concern?

You can identify several symptoms just by asking yourself some questions:

(1) *At what point in the interview did the objection come up?*

If a prospect greets you at the door and says, "I don't need anything your company makes," that might mean one thing. If the objection comes after you've shown the complete line, you have a different challenge.

"I don't need anything" is a standard way of dismissing a salesperson. If the prospect listens to your entire presentation, asks pertinent questions, then says, "I don't need anything," you can bet there's a deeper reason. And you'd better find it if you don't want to waste your time and rob yourself of potential rewards.

(2) *What mood is conveyed by the prospect's expression, tone of voice, and physical actions?*

If the customer gets up, walks toward the door, hands you your coat, and says, "See me in six months," that might say, "I'm not sufficiently sold to act now."

But if the prospect says, "Gee, I don't know . . . I might be in a better position to talk with you six months from now," it probably means, "Give me one good solid reason why I should buy today."

(3) *How many objections has this prospect thrown at me, or how many different ways has this person said the same thing?*

If the prospect shows interest but keeps throwing up smoke screens and coming back to the same objection, chances are pretty good you don't yet know the real objection.

Tactics for Spotting the Real Objection

So pinpoint it. Spot the real objection. You might try one of these tactics:

♦ *Ask for a "what-if" commitment.*

When a customer keeps coming back to price, for example, you might ask, "If I could show you how this product could save you much more than it costs, would you buy it today?"

If the prospect says, "Yes," then you've found the real issue. If the prospect responds with "I'm not sure," or a similar hedge, you're probably chasing a smoke screen.

♦ *Try a summary close, testing carefully the customer's reaction to each feature and benefit.*

You might find that the prospect is not really sold on one of the features you have presented and is using price as the smoke screen to cover up that fact.

♦ *Just ask, "Why?"*

If the prospect says, "I'm just not ready to buy," ask "Why?" You might find that the customer is not yet convinced that what you're selling will do everything that you promise.

Whatever tactic you use, target the real issue.

Get the real objection fixed clearly in your own mind and make sure you understand the problem. Then, focus on the real issue with the client.

Once the real objection is out in the open, the tension is usually relieved, and you can deal with the objection effectively.

Our research over more than two decades of consulting with many corporate sales teams has taught me one big lesson: Failure to understand the problem is the number-one reason salespeople don't handle objections properly.

Learn to pinpoint the real objection, and half the battle is won.

Be Prepared for the Objections

The second major step in handling objections is to be prepared. If you know your product, your company, and your industry, you will know that there are certain objections most customers bring up. Be prepared to deal with them effectively.

Often, if you know what objections your customer will raise, you can head them off before they surface. For example, you might say "Many of our customers ask about . . ." Then, you handle it in a way that removes all concern from the prospect's mind.

You may say something like, "I've got some great news for you: We've solved that problem, and here's how . . ."

By bringing up the issue yourself, you let the prospect know that you're not afraid to deal with it and that maybe, after all, it's not a major concern.

I'm not suggesting that when you meet with a prospect you give a list of all the possible objections to the sale. We're talking only about the most obvious or most common objections—the objections both you and the prospect know are there.

The more you prepare for the common objections, the better you will be at handling them promptly and persuasively.

Many successful salespeople prepare by dividing a sheet of paper into two vertical columns. One they title, "If the customer says . . ." Under it, they list all the objections a customer might raise. Across from that list, they write down all the answers. Then, they rehearse and even memorize that list. But they recognize that every response must be tailored to the specific customer.

Knowing in advance what you will say can be a big help in answering objections with confidence.

DON'T CREATE YOUR OWN OBJECTIONS

The pros know that to overcome objections and to get past the stalls, they have to understand the real objections. And they have to be prepared in advance to deal with the objections as they arise. They do not, however, create their own obstacles.

Here are some suggestions for salespeople who want to avoid creation of their own objections to a sale:

(1) *Make sure the customer understands what you're offering.*

Many a sale has been lost because the salesperson failed to make sure that the customer understood the products or services being offered. Many potential customers remain unconvinced because salespeople fail to make the offer clear or fail to communicate exactly what they want the customer to do. If the customer doesn't understand the product or the offer, you can be sure an objection is about to emerge. Encourage feedback from your customers so you can be sure you understand one another.

(2) *Watch for and heed the buying signals.*

Some salespeople get so caught up in what they're doing that they ignore what the customer is doing. They talk themselves right out of an easy sale. Watch for any buying signal and take advantage of it.

(3) *Suggest a specific action for the customer to take.*

Don't wait for customers to make up their own minds; they may never do it. If you have properly positioned yourself as a consultant, it'll be appropriate for you to suggest a move for your prospect. You are the expert. You know more about your prospects' needs than they do. Take control of the situation.

Many customers want a salesperson to make up their minds for them. Be nice; accommodate them. It'll make you both happy.

(4) *Don't beg for an order.*

Sometimes, hungry or inexperienced salespeople plead for orders so abjectly that they reduce their effectiveness and they hurt their chances. Customers buy for their reasons, not yours. Begging for orders just creates tension. The way to close sales is to build desire based on the customer's motivations.

To turn objections and stalls into sales, the pros know they have to get inside their prospects' heads and understand their reasons for not buying. They try to see things from their customers' points of view.

Once they have the prospect's perspective, they determine what it will take to close the sale. What is the motivating force that will move a client toward a buying decision?

When you learn to find the answers to these questions—and when you understand that objections are clues that lead to sales—you'll have selling savvy that you can use profitably and regularly.

CHECK YOUR SELLING SAVVY

I. What are the four basic reasons that people buy?

    (1) _____

    (2) _____

    (3) _____

    (4) _____

II. What are the four basic reasons that people don't buy?

(1) _____

(2) _____

(3) _____

(4) _____

III. The most important step in handling objections is:

_____

IV. What three questions can you ask to determine whether an objection is real or just a smoke screen?

(1) _____

(2) _____

(3) _____

V. List three tactics for identifying the real objection:

(1) _____

(2) _____

(3) _____

VI. What four strategies can help you avoid creating your own objections to a sale?

(1) _____

(2) _____

(3) _____

(4) _____

How to Become a
Master Closer

Every successful baseball team has in its bullpen at least one pitcher who's known as a closer.

A manager needs a good closer because he knows that the game isn't always won by the team that leads going into the ninth inning. It's won by the team that's ahead when the last out is made. A pitcher may pitch superbly for seven or eight innings, but if he can't get past the last five or six batters, he'll lose the game.

So along about the eighth or ninth inning of a close game, you'll see the manager signal to his bullpen for his master closer to come in and retire the last few batters. A good closer may be on the mound for only a few minutes. But in those few minutes, he earns his pay. In those few minutes, championships are won.

To be a good salesperson, you have to be a master closer. You can do everything else right, but if you're a clumsy closer you lose the sale. And if you don't close the sale, nobody makes money.

CLOSING OPENS THE DOOR TO SUCCESS

As a professional sales consultant, I have an opportunity to meet, observe, and work with thousands of salespeople every year.

I talk to these professionals, I listen to them, and I study what they do.

In all my years of studying the reasons successful people are successful and why unsuccessful people fail, there are three things I have never seen:

(1) *I've never seen a truly successful salesperson who could not close effectively.*

I've seen a few order-takers who started off with a bang; but they were out of business as soon as they ran out of friends.

(2) *I've never seen an effective closer who was not successful.*

If you're an effective closer, and you're diligent in calling on the right prospects, you're going to make sales.

(3) *I've never seen an effective closer whose closing techniques could not be improved.*

The good become excellent and the excellent become superb by constant improvement. We'll look at some closing techniques that will help you soar beyond your present level of performance.

It's Never Over Until You Close

One of the most famous—and accurate—sayings in baseball is attributed to Yogi Berra, the great catcher for the New York Yankees: *It ain't over till it's over.* You don't get credit for a victory until the last opposing batter goes down and you're ahead on the scoreboard.

Yogi's truism applies in sales as well as in baseball. It ain't over till it's over, which means that you don't collect your commission until you close.

A Simple Definition of Closing

Before we look at some effective closing techniques, let's get clear on what we're talking about when we say, "closing a sale."

Here's a simple but reliable definition: ***Closing a sale is clearing the way to deliver your product or service.***

On the baseball field, when the bases are empty, two men are out, and you've thrown no balls and two strikes to the third batter in the ninth, you still haven't closed. If the batter fouls the next pitch into the stands, you still haven't closed. If your next pitch narrowly misses the strike zone, you still haven't closed. You can't say you've closed the game until you've collected that last out; until you've removed the last obstacle to victory.

Similarly, you can't say you've closed a sale until your company has a green light to deliver what you've sold.

If your customer says yes, but backs out before the goods are shipped, you haven't closed a sale. If you have the order but the customer's credit doesn't clear, you haven't closed a sale. If you haven't cleared up all the details, you haven't yet closed a sale.

Closing a sale includes getting the customer to agree, getting a signed order, and getting a payment. But it's not complete until you remove every obstacle that keeps your company from delivering its goods or services.

FIVE TESTED TECHNIQUES FOR CLOSING

What are the techniques that enable the savvy salesperson to close sales regularly and consistently?

Here are five that have been tested and proved:

(1) *Take away the surprise.*

Effective closing is knowing that from the minute you make that first contact with a prospect, you begin to close the sale.

Amateur salespeople will pin down a prospect and begin the presentation. They'll quote figures, pull out samples, give demonstrations, and basically put on an informative, sometimes interesting, show.

Then, they'll fold up their flip charts, put away their props, and move in for the kill. The only problem is that the quarry isn't ready to bite the dust.

"Would you like to buy?" the amateurs ask, inwardly congratulating themselves for having asked for the sale.

Sometimes, they don't even ask. They just fold their props and go.

The prospect is surprised—sometimes even shocked—by the abrupt invitation to buy, or by the abrupt departure without an invitation.

And the salesperson is just as surprised when the prospect says something like, "I'd love to have your product, but I can't afford it."

Professionals take away the element of surprise. They regard closing as a continuous process, not an isolated event.

Everything we've covered in this book—from prospecting to handling objections—is part of the closing process.

Get Commitments Step by Step

Selling savvy is finding out up front whether a prospect has the money, the authority, and a reason to buy. It's getting a commitment from the prospect to continue, at every step of the selling process.

Most people don't like to make big decisions, so successful salespeople always give their prospects the opportunity to make several minor decisions.

To these savvy salespeople, getting a signed order is the only logical conclusion to the selling process. And taking away the surprise is the first technique they employ.

(2) *Qualify constantly.*

If you want to close successfully regularly and consistently, you have to spend your time with prospects who have the need, desire, and ability to buy your product or service.

No matter how good you are at qualifying prospects up front, nobody can bat a thousand for any length of time. And although pitchers have, on rare occasions, thrown perfect games, nobody has ever done it twice in a row. The cowboy adage is true: "There ain't a hoss that can't be rode; there ain't a man that can't be throwed." Successful salespeople acknowledge this, and look for the prospects that offer the best opportunities for successful closing.

I've found that most salespeople who believe they are poor closers are actually wasting their selling time by trying to sell to poor prospects.

One reason they waste so much time with the wrong people is that they fail to ask the proper questions along the way. They don't qualify constantly.

Keep Digging for the Right Answer

Even when you ask the right question, you may not get the right answer the first time around. It's a fact of life that people don't always level with salespeople. They don't intentionally mislead us; they just don't always tell us the whole truth and nothing but the truth.

Maybe it's because they don't want to hurt our feelings; maybe they're afraid of starting a conflict. Or perhaps they're trying to save face. It's hard for some people to admit that they can't afford something they want.

And sometimes salespeople overlook the obvious because they're so eager to make a sale.

Whatever the reason, selling savvy is assuming that there is something you may not know about the prospect until you get the final commitment.

So you keep qualifying at every step of the sales cycle.

If you determine that a prospect has no need, desire, or ability to buy, say thanks for the experience and move on to the next prospect. Why beat your brains out trying to sell to someone who cannot or will not buy?

To qualify constantly, you need to employ the next technique for closing more sales:

(3) *Find the key issue.*

J.P. Morgan, the great financier, was on to something when he said, "There are two reasons people do what they do: The real reason, and the reason they tell you."

Cutting through a prospect's smoke screen to close a sale can be like trying to find your exit on a California freeway in heavy smog. You can't close a sale in a smog.

One effective tactic for clearing away the smoke screen is to keep monitoring your prospect's commitment through preliminary screening. Ask for agreement to a condition before you proceed to the next stage of your presentation.

The prospect's reaction to certain conditions can tell you a great deal about the intention or ability to buy.

For example, you might ask, "If price were not a problem, would you be ready to proceed with this?"

If the answer is yes, move on to settle the price issue.

But if the response is, "Well, I'd have to check with Ms. Jones," then you do whatever is necessary to involve Ms. Jones in the selling process.

Any number of preliminary checkpoints can help you identify prospects who have no sincere motivation to buy. It's simply a matter of presenting to the prospect a condition that calls for a commitment to act.

Your objective is to eliminate every reason a prospect has for not buying—now. If you can do that, you have a sale. If you can't find the key issue in the prospect's mind, you don't yet have a sale.

Don't Leave the Contract for Later

If you've been selling long, I know you've had an experience similar to this:

A prospect welcomes you in, listens to what you have to say, and agrees to buy. Then, comes the stall: "Leave your contract and I'll look it over. If it's OK, I'll sign and send it back to you." Then, you wait for days and weeks and nothing happens. The order never comes.

When a prospect says, "I'll get back to you," count it as a no-sale. It might be a sale in the making, but it's not a closed sale. If you don't believe me, try depositing it in your checking account.

Clear away the smoke screen. Ask the prospect, "Is there a specific reason you don't want to go ahead with this today?"

Very often, the prospect will say something like, "Well, I'm a little short on cash-flow right now." Then, at least you know what you are dealing with.

If your question doesn't clear away the smoke screen, ask more questions until you find the key issue that must be settled.

Anyone who's been selling for a while can tell you that no matter what you do, there are times when you simply can't clear away the fog and close a sale.

As soon as you realize that a prospect's promise to "think it over" or buy later is a smoke screen for a refusal you can't overcome, graciously accept the prospect's promise, terminate the sales interview, and move on to other business. But don't kid yourself into believing you've closed the sale.

I'm not suggesting that you give up too quickly or too easily. But selling savvy is knowing when you're drilling in a dry hole and finding it out early in the process, before you've wasted a lot of time and effort. Your time is far too valuable to waste on prospects who won't buy or can't buy.

After you've penetrated the smoke screen and identified the key issue, the next step is obvious:

(4) *Settle the key issue.*

People have only four reasons for not buying. They are:

- No need.
- No desire.
- No money.
- No hurry.

If you clear away the smokescreen and discover which of the big four is keeping you from closing the sale, then you must deal with that issue.

No need means either that you have not qualified the prospect, or that you have not enabled the prospect to discover the need.

So you have to go back to probing. Remember: What matters most is not how you perceive the prospect's need; it's how the prospect perceives the need. The prospect's perception is always the reality you must deal with. If the prospect perceives no need, you can't close the sale until you've changed the perception.

No desire means that you have not found and appealed to the prospect's hot button—you have not built enough value.

Again, what matters most is not what *you* like best about what you're selling, but what the *customer* likes most.

If you discover that the key issue is no desire, go back to square one and try to discover what the prospect wants most. Then, show convincingly that the best way to fulfill that desire is with your product.

Build value, build more value, and keep building value. Remember what we said in the previous chapter: The salesperson may set the price, but it's the customer who sets the value.

The most powerful way to raise the prospect's perception of value is to focus on the most compelling reason to buy—Not your reason to sell, and not the reason most people buy, but the most compelling reason the person you're talking with has to buy.

If you discover that the key issue is *no money,* it means either that you have not qualified the prospect or that you haven't clarified the way you can help solve the money problem.

One caution here: Make sure you find out exactly what the prospect means by "no money." "I can't afford it" might mean "It's not worth the price." Or it might mean, "I think I can get it cheaper." Again, clear away the fog.

Cutting the Price Seldom Gets the Sale

It's at this point that most amateurs give away the store. They think cutting the price is the best way to move a prospect with no money to act.

Extensive research shows that cutting the price is almost never a deciding factor for the customer.

Don't give away the store. Treat the "price-is-too-high" problem as you would the issue of no desire or no need. Build more value.

If you discover that the problem really is no money, quit wasting your time and get on with finding a prospect who can afford to buy what you're selling.

Give the Prospect a Reason to Buy

The last of the big four reasons people don't buy is *no hurry.* What that means is that you haven't given the prospect a good enough reason to act *now.*

You might think you've given plenty of good reasons to buy. But, don't forget: People buy for their own reasons—not for yours.

Again, cutting the price for a limited time only is almost never the answer. Research shows that most customers believe they can buy at the cheaper price—whenever they get ready.

Search for the one most compelling reason the prospect has for acting promptly, and build on that.

That brings us to the final technique:

(5) *Pin down the close by negotiating the terms.*

This powerful technique assumes that the customer will buy and moves on to work out the details of the sale.

Remember that a sale is not closed until all the details are settled. Master closers are also master negotiators.

The key to being a good negotiator is to understand how the process works. Negotiation is a process of give and take for both parties. That suggests several things:

Negotiate All Details

It suggests that all details—not just price—have to be negotiated. I've seen salespeople lose hard-earned sales because they didn't negotiate details such as delivery dates, shipping costs, finance charges, or terms of payment.

Make sure you cover all bases.

The give-and-take nature of negotiating suggests that you need to know precisely how much maneuvering room you have available. Delaying a sale while you find out whether you can satisfy a customer's demand can cost you dearly.

Every situation is different, and only you can determine where your negotiating strengths lie with each of your prospects.

Here is another strong reason to know all you can about your company and industry. The quicker you can settle terms—without having to check back with the main office or find out what your competition can offer—the more you can head off those deadly delays.

Leave Yourself Maneuvering Room

Since negotiating is a process of giving and taking, leave yourself some maneuvering room.

For example, if you know going in that you can lower the price, don't spill the beans as soon as you walk in. That way, if the delivery date becomes a problem, you can give a price break in exchange for an agreement to ship at your convenience.

And that brings us to this point: Always get something in return for every concession you make.

If the customer wants longer to pay, charge a higher price. If the customer wants special handling, get a concession on delivery date.

That doesn't mean you should take advantage of the customer. For instance, if your company has published a price break and you don't need it for leverage, give the customer the lower price as a goodwill gesture. It can save you a problem later, when the customer finds out that you gave the price break to others.

Make Sure Everybody Wins

Another thing to remember is that good negotiators always make sure everybody wins.

That's the foundation of all successful negotiations. When you finish negotiating a sale with a customer, both of you should feel satisfied.

Too often, negotiating sales becomes a struggle that demands victory for someone. Where there's a victor, there must be a loser.

That's a very negative premise on which to establish a relationship with a client. If you leave a customer feeling like a loser, you demolish future opportunities for cross selling or repeat business.

Make it your goal always to negotiate deals that benefit both you and your prospects.

A THREE-STEP NEGOTIATING FORMULA

Now, let me share with you a three-step negotiating formula I developed to use in my training sessions. Many successful salespeople have proved its effectiveness.

(1) *Agree with the prospect on some point.*

The best place to start negotiation on any point is on common ground. You and your prospect could agree that delivery time on a product is of vital importance.

By agreeing with your prospect, you are relieving tension.

(2) *Warm up the prospect.*

Encourage the prospect to elaborate on the point on which you have just agreed. Then empathize. You might say, "I understand that getting the parts by Monday is vital to your production department."

This strengthens your trust bond with the prospect.

(3) *State your position.*

The first two steps have earned you the right to expect the prospect to understand where you're coming from. In essence, you're saying, "I understand your position. Now I would like you to try to understand mine."

This can be very powerful in getting reasonable concessions from a prospect without building resentment.

This three-step approach follows an age-old rule of negotiation, and that is to balance the process. It is a matter of give and take. If you give first—with agreement and understanding—you will be able to take later.

The most important thing to remember about closing sales is this: You have not closed a sale until you have cleared the way for your company to ship whatever you've sold.

Don't waste good sales by assuming that the customer will come through with promises about future actions.

Studies show that most buying decisions are made within 24 hours of the time the prospect receives a proposal. The longer you let a customer mull over a presentation, the lower your chances of closing that sale.

As soon as you can, without being too pushy, try to pin it down so that the prospect is saying, "I will do this specific thing at this specific time."

Structure your whole presentation so that the prospect is constantly taking some concrete action that keeps moving toward the final commitment.

Of all the characteristics shared by successful salespeople, effective, professional closing is the most crucial. It's the element that lets you take your selling savvy to the bank.

CHECK YOUR SELLING SAVVY

I. List five techniques for closing sales consistently and regularly:

(1) _____

(2) _____

(3) _____

(4) _____

(5) _____

II. List the three steps in an effective negotiating formula:

(1) _____

(2) _____

(3) _____

A Final Word

It's my firm hope that this book will become more than bedside or break-time reading for you. I want it to do for you what the efforts of so many other people have done for me.

The principles that have enabled me to achieve success as a salesperson and business consultant are basics that have been passed on to me by wise and able people whom I have known, either personally or through the things they've written or said. I want to pass them on to others as well.

I hope you will regard this book as a business tool—an instrument for carving out success in your chosen calling. Read it, certainly, but become involved in it as well.

Complete the exercises at the end of each chapter. Think about ways you can apply them in your sales efforts. The ideas they represent did not spring from daydreams. They sprang from concrete experiences of people who pursue the same career you are pursuing or are hoping to pursue.

If the book does nothing else for you, I hope it will elevate your own appraisal of who you are and what you can do. To be a professional is to earn a place of honor in your calling, whatever it might be.

People aren't born professionals. They *become* professionals by applying the principles I've written about in these pages.

The sales process is not mysterious and it is not impenetrable to the ordinary person. It's something that can be learned and followed to success.

So briefly, let us review the things we've learned in these 12 chapters, then look for ways to apply what we've learned toward the dreams we've created.

First, remember that we're dealing with a new kind of marketplace. The customers are more sophisticated, the competition is stiffer, and interactive technology is enabling people increasingly to order from a screen instead of from a person. This means that success requires more savvy than it ever did before.

To succeed, you have to become an educated professional who understands people well enough to persuade them to buy. You have to put all your training and all the skills on the front line of selling and be willing to risk—and endure—rejection and failure. You have to acquire street smarts by going into the sales arena and becoming a student of your prospects—their likes and dislikes, their motives, and their responses. You have to develop an intelligent strategy and stick with it day in and day out.

You have to acquire special knowledge and skills and use them on behalf of your customers and clients. You have to identify with your business organization and make its interests your own. But you also have to be self-managed and accountable.

You have to develop a seamless harmony between your working life and your personal life, for that complementary relationship is the hallmark of the professional in any calling. Your job must become part of who you are.

You have to position yourself as more than a generic salesperson to the people you call on. They must regard you as a professional in your field, an authority they can trust to help them solve the problems your products and services are designed to solve. You must make yourself important to these people, and you must be someone they like to see coming.

A Final Word

To achieve this position, you must first position yourself in your own mind. You have to believe that what you do is important and honorable; you have to be proud of your profession and of your position within it. You must also position yourself in your client's mind. You must come across as a person who is customer-centered, not self-centered.

You must look and act like a professional, which means that you pay careful attention to your dress and grooming. Your actions must show that you understand and respect the schedules and routines of the people you deal with. Your presence should always be a welcome asset, not an unwanted imposition.

As a professional, you help your customers and clients see the advantages of dealing with you. You handle their objections in a helpful and courteous manner. You close the sale by showing the prospect the benefits in your products and services. And you follow through by making sure the products are performing satisfactorily and that the services accomplish what they are designed to accomplish.

Professional salespeople know that they can't achieve success haphazardly. They must set goals and they must take meaningful action to achieve these goals.

They learn to distinguish between urgent tasks—things that must be done immediately to avoid dire consequences; and important tasks—things that they do systematically to move them toward their goals. They learn to minimize the urgent and emphasize the important.

They set goals that excite them, that are consistent with their purpose in life, and that enrich every aspect of their lives. They learn to set measurable goals that are ambitious but achievable. They write them down, set deadlines and develop strategies for achieving them, and then they execute their strategies.

To propel you to success in selling, you must employ the *7-P* factor: your *p*ower to *p*ersuade *p*lenty of *p*rospects to *p*urchase your *p*roducts at a *p*rofit to you. You learn to exercise patience while showing persistence without pressure; you learn that your goal is not a sale but a profitable relationship; you learn to think and act positive.

You learn to prospect intelligently. You learn to prepare carefully to put power into your performance. You learn to be perceptive; to be alert for the things affecting the progress of your sales presentation. You learn to probe with tactful questions to obtain the information you need to close a sale.

You learn to personalize your presentations for each prospect, and you look for ways to please the prospect. You find ways to prove the value of your products and services to your customer, and you persist for as long as it takes to bring a promising prospect into the sales column.

Great salespeople are great communicators. They follow the SLO process: speaking, listening, and observing. They know that they communicate with far more than words; that non-verbal messages constitute 93% of their communication. When they do use words, they speak in clear, simple, forceful language.

They know that in conversation, listening can be even more important than speaking. You learn while listening, not while talking. So they listen with the objective of understanding the message coming from the other party.

To succeed, you must learn to manage your most precious commodity: time. It's good to do things right, but it's more important to do the right things. You must direct your efforts toward ends that are both desirable and achievable. You must learn the value of developing and sticking to a schedule; of compiling and following a "to-do" list.

You must learn to make maximum use of your prime selling time and to schedule non-selling activities for other parts of the day. You must learn to organize your paper work, your travel time, your presentations, and your appointments.

Really successful salespeople develop a sense of urgency about everything they do. Every action they take is toward completion of a sale.

Professional salesmen see themselves as consultants to their customers. They find out what their customers' needs, wants, and desires are; what things are worrying them and giving them problems. Then, they offer the appropriate benefits and solutions.

184

A Final Word

To achieve this status as a consultant, you must become an expert on your field, on your company, on your products or services, on your industry, on your competition, and on your customers.

I hope you'll go back and review Chapter Eight and the questions top salespeople ask themselves and their customers, for questions can be your most powerful tools for closing sales. Learn to ask intelligent, tactful, customer-centered questions, then listen for the answers. They'll tell you what you need to know to make a sale.

One of the most important things you'll take away from this book is the knowledge that sales is a process, not a series of events. The process has to be focused, through preparation and planning. You must learn to make the broad, strategic decisions, then work out the detailed tactics that take you toward success on your sales calls.

Planning and preparation enable you to relax while giving your presentation. You don't have to struggle for words and ideas, because everything has been worked out and rehearsed in advance.

Accomplished salespeople learn to focus on their objectives and their prospects. And they learn to focus their presentations for maximum impact.

The presentation, of course, is where fortunes are made or fumbled away in the sales process. If you're a professional salesperson, you take nothing for granted. You don't expect to make a sale on every call, but you know that whether you succeed or fail depends largely upon your ability to make the prospect want what you're selling. So you look for ways to help your prospects discover pressing needs or overpowering desires. You then convince them that what you're selling will meet those needs or desires better than anything else available. You build enough value to outweigh the cost factor. And you give your prospects compelling reasons to act immediately.

Great salespeople keep the sales process moving steadily along. They qualify at every phase. And every strategy is aimed toward closing. They involve prospects by learning, through asking and listening, what specific needs or desires each person has that can be satisfied by the product they're selling. They consciously look for ways to build credibility with their prospects.

Sales pros don't regard objections as barriers to closing; they regard them as opportunities to learn what they need to do to close.

Finally, great salespeople must be master closers. They understand that the sale isn't closed until every barrier to the delivery of the goods has been removed. They learn to take care of all the small details.

They are also skilled at separating the real objections from smoke screens; at identifying the key issues and dealing with them.

When you've mastered all the techniques we've discussed, you will be entitled to be called a professional.

I hope you'll look back on the purchase of this book as a turning point in your life and career. The suggestions it contains have transformed my career and enriched my life. May they do the same for you.

For information on Nido Qubein's speeches, books, cassettes, and consulting call or write:

Creative Services, Inc.
806 Westchester Drive
P. O. Box 6008
High Point, NC 27262 USA
Telephone (336)889-3010
Facsimile (336)885-3001

NOTES

NOTES

NOTES

NOTES

NOTES

NOTES

NOTES

NOTES

NOTES

NOTES

NOTES